ON THE HOUSE

Simon Hoggart was born in 1946 and educated in Hull,
Leicester, the United States and Cambridge. He joined
the *Guardian* in 1968 and was Northern Ireland
correspondent for two years. In 1973, he became a
member of the parliamentary lobby, and the *On the
House* column, from an idea by *Punch* editor Alan
Coren, started in May 1979 – Thatcher Year One.
He is now a feature writer for the *Observer*. He says
that many of his best friends are politicians.

Australian-born John Jensen was political cartoonist of
the *Sunday Telegraph* for eighteen years and political
cartoonist of *Now!* for eighteen months (until its
demise). He has drawn for the *Tatler* and *Spectator* and
is now drawing regularly for *Punch* and illustrating
books.

Simon Hoggart
Illustrated by John Jensen

ON THE HOUSE

The Personalities and the Politics
from the Irreverent Punch Column

Pan Books London and Sydney

The author would like to thank the proprietors of *Punch* magazine
for permission to reproduce material in this book

First published 1981 by Robson Books Ltd
This edition published 1982 by Pan Books Ltd,
Cavaye Place, London SW10 9PG
Text copyright © Punch Publications 1981
Illustrations © John Jensen 1981
ISBN 0 330 26883 X
Printed and bound in Great Britain by
Hunt Barnard Ltd, Aylesbury, Bucks

Introduction

A while ago I was sent to cover a tour by a Very Senior Minister. Nothing of any importance whatever transpired on this trip, so I contented myself with sending a few light-hearted observations back to my newspaper, chiefly contrasting the culture, the customs and the poverty of the countries we were visiting with the urbane British smoothness of the Very Senior Minister. After a week or so, the VSM's public relations man came steaming up to me at a reception.

'The Minister would like to know,' he said crisply, 'if you are going to write seriously about this tour or whether you intend to persist in what he regards as childish, schoolboy humour?' I said I was sorry that he hadn't thought the jokes funny, but added that I hadn't actually criticized his boss. 'The Minister does not mind criticism. He does, however, expect to be taken seriously.'

That last remark seemed to sum it all up. Politicians really don't much mind criticism, any more than children mind being hit by mud pies. Getting them back in your face is half the fun of throwing them. But they do hate to be regarded as figures of jest. If you call a man The Worst Chancellor Of The Exchequer Since The Norman Conquest, you are in a curious way adding to his sense of self-esteem. He is an historical figure, a man with a walk-on part in destiny. Point out that he has a silly giggle or dandruff, and you make him a mere human, once more one of us.

Politicians are always telling us that we ought to concentrate on the issues, on policies and on values. Discussing public affairs in terms of personalities is, they claim, indicative of the relentless trivialization of the press. Yet it seems to me that personality is nearly always much the single most important factor in any political decision. Ted Heath's stubbornness made him challenge the miners in 1973, leading to the first 1974 General Election and the subsequent Labour Government. A mollifier, like Macmillan, would probably never have reached the same situation, and the course of British history would have been transformed. Willie Whitelaw's exaggerated sense of personal loyalty prevented him at first from standing against Ted Heath in 1975, and so contributed to the choice of Margaret Thatcher as Leader of the Conservative Party. A Tory Party under Willie would have been utterly different from the one run by Mrs Thatcher, and the situation in this country completely changed.

Similarly, Mr Foot's loyalty and Mr Healey's casual boorishness brought about the result of the 1980 Labour leadership election. If either of their temperaments had been marginally different, Mr Healey might have won, and the Labour Party would be embarked on an altered course. The success or failure of the Social Democratic Party will depend upon a host of fine judgements by its leading members – decisions which will be the result of personality quite as much as politics.

I make no claims for any of the pieces in this book which are, for the most part, the gossip and trivia which fly continually around the Palace of Westminster. But I do feel that, just occasionally, an item about Sir Keith Joseph's peculiar social habits tells us more about the way British industry was run that any number of speeches written by civil servants and delivered to Chamber of Commerce lunches. Mrs Thatcher's frequent crisp put-downs of her colleagues can help us trace the course of her Government as tellingly as all the off-the-record briefings issued from Downing Street. Policies are, of course, enormously important, but I do think that we can learn much from chit-chat as well. The fact that politicians would rather we didn't doesn't seem to me to matter very much.

And they are, at bottom, just like us. It would be absurd

to claim that MPs are a cross-section of the nation, but they do get surprisingly close to it. A few years ago (and I have bowdlerized this story) a colleague of mine was talking in the Strangers' Bar, and remarked, 'The trouble with this place is that it's full of bleeding idiots.'

An old mining MP called Bill Stone, who spent his last years drowning the pain in his lungs with pints of bitter, was sitting in a corner and overheard him. He put down his pot and remarked. 'There's a lot of bleeding idiots in t'country, and they deserve some representation.'

Precisely.

Simon Hoggart
March 1982

*The Queen opened Parliament after the Conservatives'
victory in the election of May 1979.*

A delightful sight for the public who watched the proces-
sion at the state Opening of Parliament in 1979 was the
open coach containing two of the very nicest Government
Whips, Mr John Stradling Thomas and Mr Spencer Le
Marchant, known respectively as Treasurer and Comptrol-
ler of Her Majesty's Household. They are both affable and
cheery fellows. For example Mr Le Marchant likes to
comptrol a pint of champagne each morning.

On this occasion they were waving to the cheering
crowds with their white sticks of office. Mr Stradling Thomas, spotting a lady journalist of his acquaintance, blew
her a kiss. This is, regrettably, not the way people in royal
processions usually behave. Labour Whips, who tend to
be retired trade union officials and polytechnic lecturers,
used to sit bolt upright with their sticks, looking neither
to right nor left, perhaps afraid that they would be exe-
cuted if they displayed levity. A glance down the list of
Cabinet members reveals the reason for the new, relaxed
tone. At the moment we have a government, many of
whose members regard the Queen as a social inferior.

Once again the papers are full of silly talk about the 'Heath wing' of the Conservative Party. The Heath wing consists of one man, to wit E. Heath, and nobody else, with the possible exception of Sir Timothy Kitson, and occasionally Mr Heath must have doubts about him. Contrary to public belief the silvery-haired ex-Premier can be a charming and amusing companion, with a fund of revealing anecdotes which he tells exceedingly well. Unfortunately, he has a peculiar, dry sense of humour which often sounds like, and is indistinguishable from, thoughtless rudeness.

Take, for example, Mr John Nott the accident-prone Trade and later Defence Secretary. In 1973 Mr Nott was a junior Treasury minister under Mr Heath. He was fearful that all the money which was being printed was going to cause huge inflation, so he nervously approached his leader in the lobby asking if he could speak to him briefly after the Division. Before he could say what the subject was, he was curtly cut off: 'If you want to resign, put it in writing.' Was it a joke? Mr Heath's friends say it was. Mr Nott thinks it wasn't. There is one man who will never forget and never forgive, and there are plenty of others.

The theory that there are more nobs and toffs in this new government than in any other since the war – including Macmillan's – has been strengthened this week. A useful document has come my way. It lists the phone numbers of all Tory Whips, together with a list of the places where they might be found when not actually in the House. It includes two expensive restaurants. The remainder of the list is as follows: Army & Navy Club, Bath Club, Boodles Club, Brookes Club, Bucks Club, Carlton Club, Junior Carlton Club, Guards Club, Constitutional Club, National Farmers' Club, Pratt Club, St Stephens Club, Turf Club, Cavalry Club and Garrick Club.

The only noticeable omissions are the Athenaeum, the Reform and, of course, the legendary Drones Club. Labour Whips do not have clubs. Instead they frequent Indian restaurants. One new Indian restaurant near the House

actually contains a division bell, perhaps the only one outside New Delhi to have one.

Another example of toffishness came at the recent service in Westminster Abbey to commemorate thirty years of NATO. While Labour and Liberal MPs all turned up in morning dress with striped trousers and those shiny grey ties, Lord Carrington, Mr Whitelaw, Mr Pym and the service ministers arrived in lounge suits. You have to be exceedingly upper class to do that.

In May 1979 Tony Benn announced that he would not stand for the Labour Shadow Cabinet, and so left the party's front bench.

Mr Tony Benn's first speech from the back benches was on industrial policy, and very clever it was too. Like most Benn speeches, it was calm, well reasoned, witty and logical, enlivened by occasional flashes of lunacy. He said at

Tony Benn

one point, 'I have waited 22 years to make this speech.' This is nonsense. He has been making it constantly over the past 22 years, at great length, and frequently in Cabinet. On one occasion he was rambling on, and Jim Callaghan interrupted him.

'I plead guilty, Prime Minister,' Mr Benn replied, 'and I ask for ninety other offences to be taken into consideration.'

The placing which Mr Denis Healey wins in Shadow Cabinet ballots raises a number of vital and fascinating questions. Has he enough support in the Parliamentary Labour Party? Will the British public forgive him for five years of economic failure? Will he ever get round to buying a pair of trousers which fit so he doesn't have to keep pulling them up round his belly?

Mr Healey is certainly one of the cleverest men in Parliament. But he is not, it has to be said, one of the most wildly popular. You don't see MPs coming out of his office chuckling, saying, 'Grand lad, old Denis. By heck we've had some laughs!' One feels that, as in the old joke, if he were ill the PLP would agree to send a Get Well Soon card by 154 votes to 127 with 28 abstentions.

Perhaps it is his habit of swearing at people. He is a bully, but to be fair, he bullies people his own size. He used to bully the Cabinet, which takes some nerve. A woman colleague recently interviewed him and I asked if he swore at her as much as he did at men.

'Oh no,' she replied, 'you see I had my tape recorder on. But every time I asked a question he didn't like, he made a V-sign at me.'

There is also the question of his attitude to the truth. Nobody, except a few Tories, would accuse Mr Healey of being a fibber. But, rather like those research centres where they subject airframes to extremes of heat, cold, curvature and wind to see if they break apart, Mr Healey likes to subject the truth to extremes of stress, to see what hellish conditions it can survive.

Take his famous declaration in 1974 that inflation was down to 8.4 per cent (four years later it nearly dropped to that level then started rising again).

You couldn't possibly suggest that Denis was lying, merely that what he said wasn't the absolute quintessential truth in its purest distilled state.

History, particularly political history, tends to be written about how events were shaped by great issues and astounding occurrences. In fact the reality is usually much more trivial. Mr Callaghan lost the confidence vote in March 1979 because Gerry Fitt, the MP for West Belfast, decided not to vote Labour. The principal reason he gave was that he could not vote for a government which had Roy Mason as Ulster Secretary.

According to those in the Northern Ireland office in a position to know, the ructions with Mr Mason began because Mr Mason refused to take phone calls from Mr Fitt in the middle of the night. Mr Rees, on the other hand, had always been willing to speak to him, day or night.

Perhaps if Mr Mason had taken the calls, the Labour Government would still be in office, if a great deal more tired, and with even more bags under its collective eyes.

What are absolutely the worst things about being an MP? Having to stand outside factory gates every five years, haranguing workers who only want to go home, must be one. Putting up with the kind of constituent who has wild, revolving eyes must be another. MPs have a choice between going ex-directory, which they don't like to do, or expecting phone calls about missing slates or the Communist threat at four in the morning. The late Tom Swain who, though he occasionally used to hit his fellow MPs, was a gentle man, was once found chuckling happily over a phone message from a constituent: 'Please ring re broken fire grate.'

Another problem is braving the bores of the bars, those MPs who want to talk only about their select committee

14

on rat infestation, or who have a vague but extremely lengthy memory of the early days of Labour history. These people can usually be shut up by asking in a plonking voice: 'Just who the hell was this Keir Hardie bloke?' But of all the crosses an MP has to bear, I suspect the worst is the London cabbie.

Climb into a taxi at the members' cab rank, or pick one up in the West End, and before he has even swung into the traffic just in front of the speeding bus he has the glass partition open and is asking his first question, 'You an MP, then?' The correct answer to this, even if you are Harold Wilson himself, is 'No'. Any answer which even hints that you might once have met a girl whose father knew an MP, leads to a tirade which lasts from Charing Cross Road, throughout the two-hour drive round Trafalgar Square, and all the way down Whitehall.

The trouble is that not only do MPs discuss matters of urgent interest to taxi-drivers, such as taxation, prices and most of all immigration, but they are also nominally in charge of the fare structure in the Metropolitan area. In fact this is usually worked out by the Home Office, and I can't recall when it was last debated or voted upon, but nevertheless taxi-drivers hold MPs responsible for their permanent penurious condition. (But why, since they are so poor, are there literally hundreds of chaps on motor-scooters doing the 'knowledge' around town every week-end? All these people are presumably putting in months of time to become cab drivers.)

Catching a cab to the House the other day from Oxford Street, after my firm 'No' to the first, inevitable, question, the driver said with relish, 'I had one in my cab the other day. Gave him a right caning, I did.'

Then he recounted blow by blow the conversation, the feeble replies the wretched legislator had given, his own stunning ripostes. I began to feel deep pity for the poor MP, and hoped that it was some rich Tory with interests in the arms trade.

Problems for the Labour Party over their grotesquely expensive building in the Walworth Road, in South London. It's extremely inconvenient, and nobody wants to move there. In an effort to raise morale, it was decided that the new building should have a name. Unfortunately, so great are the rivalries within This Great Movement of Ours, that there was not the remotest chance that the comrades could ever agree on any person to name it after. 'Ramsey Macdonald House', for example, would not have given the effect intended.

So the party's Treasurer, Norman Atkinson, has circulated a private letter to the National Executive, suggesting the neutral name of Forum House. Unfortunately, this is also the name of a well-known magazine in which people describe their sex lives in alarming detail, so that will probably have to be rejected. Perhaps something with a slightly more dated air would suit the old-fashioned Labour Party: Lilliput House, or Esquire Buildings maybe.

Westminster is a cruel place. After a shouting match between Leo Abse and Enoch Powell over Ulster and whether Britain should stay there, someone remarked that the two men held each other in mutual contempt.

Another MP added: 'Yes, and they're both right.'

One of the delights of the European elections and the low turnout was the suffering it caused the Euro-bores. Whatever your views on British membership there is something peculiarly awful about Euro-bores, their assumption of greater moral virtue than the rest of us have, the way they can discuss goats' cheese intervention prices in four languages.

Recently a colleague from *The Times* was attending a stupendously boring Euro-reception given by the Liberals. Up hove one of the great Euro-fanatics, Lord Gladwyn, who used to be called Mr Gladwyn Jebb and was once our Ambassador to Paris. He immediately harangued the *Times* man, for some unfathomable reason in fluent German. After fifteen minutes he said something in a clearly interrogative tone which required an answer. The *Times* man panicked for a moment, then said in English, 'I don't know, I think you just go to the bar and help yourself.' Apparently Gladwyn's fury was gratifying to see.

I gather that he did not make much more of an impression on General de Gaulle. The late Sir Peter Kirk, who was leader of the British Tory delegation, had a saying: 'Le raison pour le "Non", c'etait le Gladwyn Jebb.'

More about the toffs' party: no fewer than four of the 60 successful Conservative candidates in the European elections were peers of the realm. My arithmetic may be wrong, but I make that approximately 2,732 times the national average.

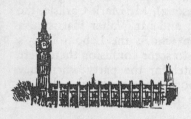

MPs began grumbling about Mrs Thatcher's Prime Ministerial style early.

The word from the Cabinet is that the most dynamic woman of all, the Prime Minister, is in firm command. Sturdy ministers with years of political combat training quail at her every word. When she visits the Members' Dining Room hordes of sycophants cluster round her, anxiously hanging on her lightest utterance. One Tory MP said that talking to her was to be trapped, like a rabbit in headlamps.

Apparently the knack is to let her start the conversation. This will often be upon some surprisingly banal topic, such as school holidays or the weather. You then agree firmly

17

with her, perhaps expanding on her remarks, but never letting the faintest hint of controversy creep into what you say, e.g. 'Oh I don't know, I think you can often lay a patterned carpet with striped wallpaper.' This is what the Americans call a no-no, and will be remembered and held against you.

The Knighthood awarded by Mrs Thatcher to Mr Jasper More, who used to be the Tory MP for Ludlow, brings to mind the extraordinary events which surrounded a parliamentary delegation to New Zealand some years ago. Before this startling tale can be told it should be firmly asserted that all the characters are committed heterosexualists, who have probably never even been to the National Liberal Club.

The delegation consisted of Mr More (now, delightfully, Sir Jasper as in the famous song), Mr Mark Carlisle, the former Education Secretary, and Mr Walter Harrison, a plain-spoken Wakefield man who is the Labour Party's Deputy Chief Whip. Owing to some confusion there were only two rooms in the hotel for the party when they arrived. Since one of the rooms contained a double bed, it was thought appropriate that the two Conservatives should sleep together.

The following morning Walter Harrison, disgustingly bright and breezy as always, descended with spring in step for breakfast. There he encountered Mark Carlisle, hollow of cheek, saggy of jowl and puffy of eye. A series of low moans floated across the toast rack towards Harrison. Now and again a butter knife would drop from lifeless fingers. The crow's feet under the Carlisle eyes made it look as if Hitchcock had used his face for the set of *The Birds*.

'It's Jasper,' croaked Mr Carlisle. 'He snores. I didn't get a wink of sleep all night.'

The sympathetic Harrison wasted no time. 'Leave it to me,' he said. 'I'll sleep with him tonight.'

And so many hours later Mr Harrison went up to bed,

climbed in, snapped off the light, rolled over towards Mr More and said, 'Give us a kiss, Jasper.' Mr More did not close his eyes all night and Walter Harrison slept the sleep of, if not the just, the extremely devious.

Mr Heath's first book had the gnomic title: *Sailing – A Course Of My Life*. He was joking that the next one might be about cookery. It could be called *Cooking – Three Courses Of My Life*.

I was sorry to hear of a heated argument between Robin Day and Lord Harris, who used to be a Home Office minister and is now chairman of the Parole Board.

'The Parole Board is,' Day remarked bitterly, 'the last Quango for Harris.'

Summer – even the crummy apology of our summers – means that much of the business of the House of Commons is conducted on the Terrace. It is a delightful place, particularly in the cool evening after a long and hot day. At night pleasure boats with throbbing discos swerve across the river in the hopes of giving their passengers a glimpse of the Prime Minister or some famous drunk. In the dark one can barely make out who is with his wife and who his mistress. Mr John Stonehouse used to bring his secretary, Miss Buckley, to the Terrace to go through the mail; Mr George Brown, when Deputy Prime Minister, was present at many a convivial session there. One lobby correspondent, with hopeless ambitions to be a cricketer, used to bowl empty wine glasses into the river with a feeble attempt at leg spin.

Mr Gerry Fitt, the member for West Belfast, used to sit on the wall and salute the passing tourists on the river with his glass of gin and tonic. 'And it's all free!' he would yell at them. Sadly it isn't, though the House remains one of the cheapest places in London to drink.

Mr William van Straubenzee, the MP for Wokingham, once puzzled a new Tory colleague by solemnly waving at

the pleasure boats as they passed. He explained that there were two or three hundred people on each boat and, by the law of averages, there should be one of his constituents on every other boat. If they thought he was waving at them they would be delighted, tell their friends, and there were a few more Conservative votes. To van Straubenzee's delight the new member believed all this rubbish and could later be seen standing and waving at each boat as it passed.

There was, no doubt, rejoicing throughout the nation at the news that the handsome, young, dynamic MP for Thanet, Mr Jonathan Aitken, had finally become engaged to be married. For the thousands of admirers the news will have made up for the fact that the Prime Minister chose not to give him an appointment in her Government – in spite of the fact that Mr Aitken was at one time an assiduous courter of the charming Carol Thatcher.

Or it could, of course, have to do with incidents which surrounded a visit Mr Aitken paid in 1975 to Saudi Arabia, where he had business interests. Mrs Thatcher has a memory which makes an elephant look scatter-brained and an incident from a mere four years ago is still as fresh in her mind as that morning's breakfast.

Mr Aitken's visit to Saudi Arabia coincided with the Tory leadership contest, and the local English-language newspaper asked his opinion of the various candidates and their views on the Middle East situation. Of Mrs Thatcher Mr Aitken said, 'I wouldn't say she was open minded on the Middle East so much as empty headed. For instance, she probably thinks that Sinai is the plural of sinus.'

None of this would have mattered except that *Private Eye* got a copy of this interview and printed it after Mrs Thatcher's election. Mr Aitken was approached by a grim-faced Airey Neave who inquired whether the quotes in *Private Eye* were true. If so, she would like an apology.

'Of course, I'll drop her a line,' said Aitken, explaining that it had only been a light-hearted pleasantry in the first place.

'That will not do,' said Neave, his face as set and grim as ever. 'She requires you to apologize in person.'

'Of course,' Aitken replied, 'I'll have a word next time I bump into her.'

'Nor will that do,' said Neave. 'She has asked me to tell you that she will see you in the Lobby tonight, after the Division at 10.15. She will be wearing green.'

History books talk about the passage of this or that act, the failure of such a bill, the thunderous debates and speeches which lead to the changes in our constitution, our laws and the very structure of our society. What they seldom write about is what really happens, the details of parliamentary life which actually determine legislation, and, in the case of one recent event, the way a conveniently situated lavatory saved our precious civil liberties or else took us one more step down the road to anarchy.

The occasion was the debate on the West Midlands County Council Bill, a 'private' bill, or rag-bag of measures promoted by a single person or institution, in this case, naturally enough, the West Midlands County Council. At one stage in its life this bill contained a clause, requested by the police, requiring the organizers of demonstrations and marches to give the police several days' prior notice. Various left-wing and libertarian MPs were opposed to this on the grounds that it would effectively prevent 'spontaneous' demonstrations and increase the control of the police over free speech and public assembly. Various right-wing and unlibertarian (to be fair, the Right uses the term 'freedom' which is generally speaking the opposite of the leftish term 'liberties') MPs wanted the clause put back in. If it had gone to a vote, the Right would certainly have won.

However, it never went to a vote. A time limit is set for the discussion of amendments and on the night in question the time limit was at 10.45. Any amendments not voted on by that time automatically fell.

A few minutes before 10.45, the vote which preceded

the one concerning demonstrations was going its normal way, with MPs dutifully queueing through the division lobbies, which are handsome, wide, book-lined corridors, with fireplaces, writing desks and, as it happens, lavatories. It became clear to the Left that the vote was going to be completed before 10.45, thus leaving time for the division on demonstrations to take place.

Back in the Chamber the minutes ticked by. The Right began to realize that something was happening. Mrs Jill Knight demanded action. The Speaker did what a Speaker's gotta do. He despatched one of the Serjeant at Arms' deputies to find out what was happening and to get the division completed.

When he arrived, what he found was a line of twelve Labour MPs queuing up to use the lavatory. He stood there fingering his sword, provided so that he can break up fights between MPs and used less often than one might imagine, and said, 'Mr Speaker has instructed me to ask honourable members to clear the Lobby.' This was greeted with the obvious remark, 'We're waiting to use the lavatory,' and, *sotto voce*, 'Piss off.' Mr Skinner pointed out that there was someone within a cubicle inside the lavatory. The division could not be said to be complete until he too had walked past the clerks' desk and so voted. The Serjeant at Arms' deputy went inside to have a look.

Meanwhile, back in the Chamber, Labour MPs were pointing out that the business of the House could not continue since there was nobody in the Serjeant at Arms' chair to keep order. By this time at the end of the whole débâcle, it was past 10.45 and too late for the amendment to be taken. In such a way are the mighty tablets of the law engraved.

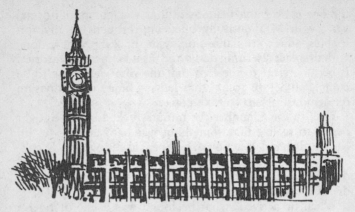

Early in the life of the administration, his colleagues began to be worried about the then Secretary of State for Industry.

Is Sir Keith Joseph showing the strain too much? Is he going over the top? There are plenty of Conservative MPs who think that the Industry Secretary might not last the course. He might suffer an attack of Lack Of Nervous Fibre and be obliged to stand down before the economic miracle he has worked so slavishly to promote has actually occurred.

To be fair to the Guru, those nearest to him do not think so. They say he is exactly as normal, which is to say exceedingly tense and twitchy. And there must be much truth in what they say. If Sir Keith were to be relaxing in a deckchair in his back garden, a cooling drink by his side, and a favourite book (say Hayek's *Road to Serfdom*) on his lap, he would still be as jittery as he always is. He has the relaxed, carefree attitude to life of a mother hen. He could no more take things easy than he could win Wimbledon. He is a sort of Woody Allen without the jokes.

What he does is to fill all his spare time, like Polyfilla, with improving activities such as reading. Richard Adams, the *Watership Down* man, used to work for him in his

Civil Service days, and encountered the minister in his office, ploughing through the *Cambridge Modern History*. Joseph explained that he read a lot of biography, and could not hope to appreciate it fully without the historical background.

Now he has spread the idea to his civil servants. The more senior of them were presented with a reading list, containing many books by divers hands including several by Sir Keith himself. They were to work through the list in order to acquaint themselves with his political and economic philosophy. A press colleague came by a copy of the list, and being a diligent chap decided that he too ought to learn about our new masters by starting on it.

At the top was Adam Smith's *Wealth of Nations*, and my colleague, who had not read this for many years, went to Dillon's University Bookshop to buy it. The assistant in the economics department expressed some surprise. 'Do you know,' she said, 'in all the time I've worked here nobody has asked me for that book. Now you're the second today!'

My colleague asked carefully, 'Was the first chap a sort of middle-aged fellow with a dark suit, possibly a bowler hat, and a black briefcase with EIIR stamped on it?'

The girl's jaw dropped. 'How on earth could you have known that?' she asked. No doubt similar scenes took place all over London as civil servants scampered to keep up with Sir Keith.

My favourite Sir Keith quote came some time ago while he was visiting a bird sanctuary. 'How on earth do the birds know it is a sanctuary?' he asked.

Wild horses, even wild dogs, could not drag from me the name of the Liberal MP who was going about suggesting that the ideal choice for a special emissary to go to Zambia to assess the Queen's safety from rocket attacks would be Jeremy Thorpe. But here is a clue. It is the same man who, before Thorpe resigned as leader, went around saying, 'We've solved our leadership crisis. John Curry is going to be leader, and Jeremy is taking up ice skating.'

Mention of Norman St John-Stevas reminds one that he really is a quite splendid dresser. His choice of four different shades of purple for shirt, tie, buttonhole and complexion gives him the air of a rather High Church bishop without the mitre – though that may come. At a Shadow Cabinet meeting not all that long before the election, he announced that he had to leave early, since he had a function to attend. 'But Norman,' the Leaderene interposed, 'I'm going there as well, and I'm not leaving the meeting.'

'Ah, but Margaret,' he replied, 'it takes me so much longer to change than you.'

(*This witty remark was indeed made by Mr St John-Stevas. But I learned later that the joke was first told about Disraeli and Queen Victoria.*)

Peter Jay's mordacious warnings about the bleak future of

NATO again remind us of the perennial question: is our former ambassador to the USA a Martian? I ask not rhetorically, but in a genuine spirit of enquiry.

The theory was first suggested by James Fenton, who used to be the political sage on the *New Statesman* before that organ was given over entirely to graphs. Fenton pointed to the thick fleshy lips, the unnaturally high intelligence, and suggested that Jay was controlled by a panel of knobs and dials set into his back.

I believe it is true that Jay is of Martian origin, but that it is wrong to suppose that he is controlled by buttons and levers. After all, Martians are much cleverer than us, or else they could not have arrived here in such large numbers. What happens is that they are given exceedingly efficient and intensive training courses to teach them how to be faultless and brilliant examples of whichever people they are to be sent amongst. Kissinger was a fairly obvious Martian: Bjorn Borg is another.

But of course, however skilful the course, there are bound to be omissions, little mistakes that to us trained Martian-spotters are entirely revealing.

The other day I attended a dinner party at which an American diplomat was talking about his visit to Ascot. He had hired his suit, he said, at 'Moss Brothers'. Suppose during the War that someone with an English accent and public school manner had told you he had been to Moss Brothers and not to Moss Bros, you would have known he was a German spy as surely as if he had worn a spiked helmet, a monocle and duelling scars.

Similarly Jay accidentally gave away his extra-terrestrial origins at a cricket match in which I found myself playing, or at least unwillingly fielding on the boundary, some years ago. Like Jay, I was playing for the *Times* team against a local side in Sussex. The home side made a decent total, our first three batsmen made modest but satisfactory scores, then Jay arrived at the crease. He was brilliant, dazzling, beautiful to behold. As each ball was despatched towards the ropes, Jay could be seen in wonderful poses which could only have been copies off old cigarette cards of Constantine and Len Hutton. In no time at all, he scored all the runs, the *Times* were easy winners, and nobody else got to the wicket. That was the fatal thing they forgot to teach him in Martian school: an English gentleman invariably knows when to give an easy catch so that everyone else has a chance to bat.

The column spotted the notorious Lothario of thés dansants early.

Something will have to be done. I fear, about Mr Geoffrey Dickens, the new Tory MP for Huddersfield West. A large man, closely resembling his namesake's Fat Boy, Mr Dickens is in the habit of throwing around his considerable weight. He tends to arrive with a pile of frightful speeches and instruct the press to take notice of them. On one occasion he burst in and demanded photographers to attend on him: three of his constituents were on the terrace and wanted a picture. He clearly did not realize (a) that photographers are not allowed in the House of Commons and .(b) that if they were, they would have much better things to do than to further Mr Dicken's political career.

Few MPs ever suffer from offending the press, however, but one man they cannot afford to cross is Mr Walter Harrison, the Labour Deputy Chief Whip. Unsung and unheard-of outside Parliament, Mr Harrison has been running the place for some years now, and has not seen the 1979 election result as any reason for stopping. Among other useful tasks he performs is the allocation of office space for members. Since there is a great shortage of this commodity, Mr Harrison's position is a powerful one.

Mr Dickens made the mistake of haranguing him about the inadequacy of his accommodation. What, he demanded, was Harrison going to do about it? Harrison snarled back, and a lasting enmity was born.

Some days later Dickens was waiting outside the voting lobby being used by Labour for a division, chatting to two colleagues. They were causing a slight obstruction and MPs hurrying to vote had to push around them. Harrison waited for the crucial moment, swept forward, and caused all three to step aside into the Labour lobby. At that instant the Speaker called 'Lock the Doors!', burly policemen performed their time-honoured duty, and the three Tories were trapped inside, obliged by procedural law to cast their vote with Labour. 'Ah, my three pretty butterflies,' beamed Harrison through the door, then to Dickens, 'I told you I'd get you, you —!'

Things began to look bad for the government even in the early months.

What a woebegone sight Mrs Thatcher's ministers present these days! Not all of them, of course: her Treasury ministers look as cheerful as Sweeney Todd when another customer is despatched next door. The ones who are looking so miserable, the ones who are actually driven to denying that they are about to resign ('The trouble is that you can't resign after only three months, it just isn't done,' one said the other day after another perfectly horrible Cabinet meeting) are the weedy-wets, the liberal-minded Tories who thought that between them they and the Civil Service could calm down the worst excesses of the Prime Minister and the Mad Monk – their affectionate nickname for Sir Keith.

How wrong they have proved so far to be! It's as if the Hubert Laneites from the *Just William* stories had taken over, only to discover that Violet Elizabeth Bott was running the show. If they don't do what she says, then she will 'thcweam and thcweam' until she's sick, and then they'll be sorry.

But even this image wavers and dissipates in the mind, and we see instead the ferocious headmistress, beating down recalcitrant pupils by the sheer force of her will. It is a quite extraordinary fact that she used to, literally, wag her finger at Jim Callaghan when he was Prime Minister. Prime Ministers may be bossed around by their wives, their Cabinet Secretaries, even, in the case of Sir Harold, by their shorthand-typists. To be lectured like an ignorant schoolboy by the Leader of the Opposition must be galling in the extreme.

The weedy-wets are wringing their hands about these public spending cuts and the monstrous interest rates which are helping to ruin what is left of British industry. It is pointed out to them, gently and with sympathy, that all this was in the Tory manifesto on which they were happy to fight and win an election. Ah, they say, but all sorts of rubbish finds its way into manifestos, and ours didn't contain anything about mass unemployment, dole queues, soup kitchens and so forth. To which the answer is that they knew she said she was going to do all this. Why didn't they believe her?

Meanwhile, the Big Four, her *consiglieri*, are currently running the country. They are Sir Geoffrey Howe, the Chancellor, the Chief Secretary to the Treasury, Mr John Biffen, the Industry Secretary, Sir Keith Joseph, and the Trade Secretary, Mr John Nott. They are all civilized and

thoughtful men. Behind them, though not yet in the Cabinet, is their hit man, Mr Nigel Lawson, the Financial Secretary to the Treasury. If this government were the secret police in an East European state, it is Sir Geoffrey and Mr Biffen who would offer you the cigarettes, the coffee and the philosophical remarks: 'Vot a tragedy zat our two countries should be at var ... togezzer, who knows?' while Mr Lawson would come in and slam you in the kidneys. The weedy-wets absolutely hate him. They say that he invents all these appalling cuts and then sells them to the Big Four. The Big Four tip the wink to the PM, and she announces the various horrors. Usually Prime Ministers 'take the voices', which means that without having a formal vote they assess the views of the Cabinet and come to the appropriate conclusion. She doesn't. She knows that the weedy-wets are in a majority, and therefore she knows perfectly well what they think. So she announces what she intends to do and there is an end to it.

Sometimes she is wrong. They told her what would happen over MPs' pay, but she went ahead anyway. Lord Carrington appears to have put her right over the boat people. The question now is: how much longer will this go on, or will the weedy-wets finally revolt?

Elections are one of the few times that politicians make real contact with the public.

A canvasser was working during the European elections in North Kensington. She arrived at a house, introduced herself and asked if she could count on the owner's support. 'I'm very glad you called,' said the man angrily. 'I have a complaint!'

'Oh, you have a complaint,' she said, her eyes glancing down at the canvassing card, 'do you, Mr Portnoy?'

Walter Brown, the Labour Party's Deputy National Organizer, was soliciting votes in Surbiton during the last election. He knocked on a door and a man's voice said, 'Come in, I'm in bed.' When he got in, he found the man in bed with a woman.

'I've always voted Labour, you can count on me,' the man said.

'And your wife?' asked Mr Brown.

'Oh, this isn't my wife, this is Mrs Jones from number 6,' the man said.

One of the most popular characters in Parliament is Mr Spencer Le Marchant, Tory MP for High Peak, and until he was sacked a Government Whip.

There are those, it should be said, who are misled by Mr Le Marchant's slow and affable manner into thinking that he is – how can we put it? – not the leading intellectual giant in politics. They point unkindly to the fact that when he goes home to his constituency on the train he has a big label placed round his neck saying 'Please Put This Whip Out At Buxton'. They are rude about the way that during one of his rare speeches to the House (Whips, by custom, do not speak), his remarks were entirely in pidgin English. This was because he had recently made an official visit to Papua-New Guinea, and he had picked up the patois there.

Again, carping and cavilling critics sometimes cite a conversation he had with a colleague shortly after returning from a summer holiday big game fishing off Florida. What, he was asked, did this sport consist of? Well, he replied, you caught the fish, the marlin or whatever, and then you threw it back. Aha, said his companion, there Spencer you may have hit on the answer to the cod war! Spencer thought long and hard, knitted his brows, and then illumination struck. 'Oh no, it's quite different, you see. . .'

Mr Le Marchant is also an extraordinarily generous man. Not only is he quite enormously rich, but he keeps winning vast quantities of money on the races. If he asks you what you would like to drink, and you carelessly say 'a pint, please' you are likely to get a pint mug of champagne.

All this is by way of prelude to describing how Mr Le Marchant, through a quick-wittedness not suspected by all his colleagues, saved an important part of the Government's programme. It also illustrates once again the extraordinarily haphazard way our Parliament proceeds, and the manner in which bills and orders go through as much by good luck as judgement.

Some order concerning industry was to be debated, but it had been misdrafted and had to be sent back. The debate was postponed, but nobody bothered to tell the Junior Employment Minister, Mr Patrick Mayhew, who was due to start the next debate on an Employment order, something to do with redundancies.

Mr Mayhew was not present to move the order. Labour MPs shouted, 'Where is he?' The Speaker dropped a heavy hint, pointing out that anybody could actually move the thing, and finally Spencer Le Marchant lumbered to his feet, no slight task since he was being tugged down by a bemused Willie Whitelaw at the time. Having struggled free from the grip of the Deputy Prime Minister Mr Le Marchant uttered only his second speech in five years, consisting of the words 'I beg to move'. By this time, through various other delays, Jim Prior was produced to make the speech on the order – a subject about which he knew absolutely nothing.

At this point, Labour could have destroyed the hapless

Prior by letting him flounder totally out of his depth. They could even have stopped the order going through by demonstrating the Minister's total ignorance. Instead, like the thick-headed buffoons they so often are, they kept interrupting him with points of order. Each time Prior sat down, civil servants were able to pass him more of the notes they had prepared for Mr Mayhew's speech. Prior made a perfectly able speech himself, and the order went through with a majority of 77, thanks to a few clots on the Labour side and the unexpected verve and brilliance of Mr Spencer Le Marchant.

The House is deserted every summer, and 1979 was no exception.

The House of Commons changes during the recess. Like a stage when the curtains are drawn and the props dismantled, large parts of it simply disappear. Seemingly half the floorboards are raised, turning the corridors of power into hazardous catwalks, as scores of workmen lay wide, impressive-looking pipes. These are something to do with the new air-conditioning system. While the United States, which actually has hot weather, is learning to live without frozen air, the House of Commons, which is always in recess for two of the three summer months, is having it piped in regardless of oil crises and Arabs. Huge quantities of furniture are moved from one place to another. Massive brown Chesterfields displaced from the Smoking Room line the Ways and Means corridor like slumbering hippos. Whole staircases are blocked off by multi-tiered piles of chairs. Vast rolls of carpet lie in wait to trip the hurrying visitor.

In the Members' Lobby, sealed off from an inquisitive public by acres of polythene sheeting, they are working on two stone plinths which stand on either side of the exit towards the Central Lobby. On one, it is said, Clement

Enoch Powell

Attlee will shortly be raised. He will join Churchill, Balfour, Joe Chamberlain and other petrified politicians gazing out on the scurrying and scheming which swirls around the lobby when the House is sitting.

The other plinth seems to be unaccounted for. One suggestion is that it should be devoted to the Unknown Lobby Correspondent. The sculptor would capture a facial expression devoted to world-weary cynicism and servility in equal measure, a pile of scruffy papers would be in his hand, and at his feet would stand the Eternal Gin and Tonic.

In the midst of the works, by the Commons rifle range, there was a large colourful notice headed THINK METRIC. Underneath was a drawing of a large foot, and the legend: 'This is not a foot. It is 300 millimetres.' Someone had scrawled underneath: 'And who is going to 300 millimetres the bill for all this load of trash, then?'

In the recessional gloom, we met Enoch Powell in a lift. He had, he said, been writing to a vicar who had criticized the fact that he was to give a series of talks in a church.

'If I am in breach of the laws of the Church, then it is hard luck on Jesus Christ,' he said. Mr Powell is a practising Christian. What could he possibly have meant?

He was dressed in an extraordinarily baggy set of tweeds, with a battered countryman's cloth cap on his head, altogether equipped for a hearty walk through the Shires in the dead of winter. Why was he dressed in this manner, we enquired?

'Because I am going on holiday,' he explained. And where was he going, we called as the lift stopped and he rushed towards the car. 'To Spain!' he cried as he disappeared. One hopes he will remember to take at least the cap off when he gets to the beach.

I see that Mr Willie Whitelaw is being misquoted again. Whenever the newspapers mention our ebullient Deputy Prime Minister they bring to mind his famous remark made during the October 1974 election on the subject of

Labour ministers. 'They are going about the country stirring up apathy,' or rather what he actually said, which was: 'They are going about the country stirring up complacency' – a slightly different thing, and, in an intriguing metaphysical way, almost meaningful.

But, of course, this remark is only one of scores made by Mr Whitelaw in similar vein. They don't indicate that the Home Secretary is stupid; indeed quite the opposite, since they show that his brain works faster than his tongue. In most politicians, the reverse is true.

In another of the press conferences in the October '74 election he was asked about morale in the Conservative

Party, which in the (correct) view of us assembled hacks was pretty low. According to Whitelaw it had never been higher. (You can always tell when Willie is fibbing; he looks so awfully glum.) How, we persisted, did he know? How could he judge?

'Well,' he replied. 'I have the thermometer in my mouth and I am listening to it all the time!'

The beauty of Willieisms, as we call them, is that they do tend to stop all further questioning. I once saw him end a conversation with a persistent lady journalist by plonking, apropos of absolutely nothing, the following rubric: 'So there it is, there you are, and there you have it!'

Offered a drink, he will ask for 'a little whisky', and asked to elaborate will explain, 'When I say I would like a little whisky, I mean I would like a large whisky, thank you very much.'

On another occasion he saw off those who suggested he might not feel entirely committed to Tory immigration policy. 'Those who say that I am not in agreement with the policy are, rightly or wrongly, quite wrong.'

My personal favourite question-stopper was at a press conference in Northern Ireland. It was the first he had held since being appointed Ulster Secretary two days before, and it had been hurriedly arranged in a reception room at Aldegrove Airport, Belfast. Willie had barely time to get briefed, and certainly had no experience of the extreme and admirable persistence of Irish journalists when they get a subject between their teeth.

The topic for that day was para-military parades, and in particular those held by Mr William Craig's Vanguard movement. For most of us who knew Mr Craig for a personally shy and gentle man with an interest in clothing and boating, these parades with their echelons of black-jacketed motor-cyclists and streaming banners were merely ludicrous.

To the Roman Catholics they were designed to threaten, they must have been terrifying. What, the journalists wanted to know, was the new Ulster Secretary going to do about these parades? Was he going to invoke the Public Order Act to prosecute their organizers? If not, why not?

Willie clearly hadn't been acquainted with this problem and was far too wily a bird to commit himself to any possibly disastrous course of action, so he fended off the questions for ten minutes until they became impossible to stem. He drew himself up to his impressive full height and announced: 'I have always said it is a great mistake ever to pre-judge the past.'

That stopped the questions.

The last Irish Prime Minister but one always got an unfairly bad press here.

Poor Jack Lynch! The Irish Prime Minister is most unfortunate to find himself reviled by British newspapers and treated rather like a particularly obtuse and obstinate schoolboy by Mrs Thatcher. Britain might at least be grateful for the fact that Mr Lynch is in office at all. He is a fairly sick man, and is thought to be hanging on only in the hope of dishing the chances of his heir apparent, Mr Charles Haughey. Mr Haughey, who was once fired by Mr Lynch for his connection with arms running, is not a particularly nice man and would not be good news for Britain. Altogether we ought to thank Mr Lynch for keeping him out, and not attack the poor fellow for finishing his holiday in Portugal, which was no doubt richly deserved.

The other point is that no Irish politician can appear to be the tool of Britain, whatever the situation. Irish history is all terribly recent, fearfully immediate: it's as if we had people still alive who had fought at the Battle of Hastings. Politicians seen to approach Mrs Thatcher with fingers clenched round forelock, muttering 'Anyt'ing you say, Ma'am, at all, at all' would be out on their ear pretty fast.

It is extraordinary that two countries so close together,

sharing the same language and with so much history and ancestry in common, should understand each other so poorly. The Irish view of an Englishman is basically of an arrogant, upper-class idiot. The English view of the Irish tends to be of a feckless, lower-class idiot. Yet the Irish image of themselves tends to be much closer to Jack Lynch: a quiet, reflective, undemonstrative sort of chap, gently puffing his pipe in the corner of the bar. The difficulty with this view is that it makes Mr Lynch appear more torpid than he is, and contributes to the British view of him as a wet and timid incompetent.

Many years ago, when Ted Heath was Prime Minister, he organized a meeting at Chequers between Lynch and Brian Faulkner, then Prime Minister of Ulster. It was the first such meeting to have taken place in Britain since partition. The talks went badly; neither side appeared ready to make any concessions, and in the early evening,

MR LYNCH IS IN RECEPTION, SIR — HAVING A PADDY!

the Irish party indicated that they had to leave for a formal dinner at their Embassy in London.

At this point an official turned up and whispered in Heath's ear that Downing Street had laid on a case of Lynch's favourite whiskey, known as 'Paddy'. Would it not be a courtesy to offer the Irish a drink? Heath agreed, and Lynch's party accepted with speed. The drinks continued for several hours, the dinner at the Embassy was cancelled and, for the first time, the talks began to get somewhere.

The following morning Lynch appeared to continue the talks, and Heath jovially explained that there was a little of the whiskey left. Would he, ho ho, like another drink? To his astonishment Lynch eagerly accepted and the talks again progressed well.

Westminster has its own cast of characters, many of them unknown to the public.

Mr Michael English, the Labour MP for Nottingham West, is one of those Westminster institutions little known to the outside world but quite as famous as, say, Jim Callaghan within the House of Commons. For one thing, he is always there. He has always been always there. Marriage and the birth of a beautiful baby daughter had not changed the habits of a lifetime. Other MPs go on holidays, lecture tours, and fact-finding visits. Mr English sits in Parliament. He has only two interests in life: House of Commons procedure and the Committee on Public Expenditure which until recently he chaired. Often the two interests coincide. Many years ago, before he met his wife, he was spotted at a party in Chelsea, an attractive young woman on either side, both of whom appeared to be listening to him intently. As a colleague passed him he cried, 'Ah! I was just explaining to Pat and Susan (or whatever they were called) that my committee's fourth report on public expenditure had a first-rate press, with the possible exception of the *New Statesman*.'

He is a stickler for procedure in all its forms. For instance if he sees somebody he doesn't know using some Commons facility to which he is apparently not entitled, he will approach them and say, 'I don't think we've been introduced.' One very senior BBC man shut him up by saying. 'Oh yes, we have, about thirteen years ago. I think you were wearing the same suit.'

He is a great one for comparing obscure paragraphs of even more obscure documents. These, it will turn out, reveal a slight shift in government policy towards duty on kangaroo-meat imports from non-EEC countries. His favourite phrase is: 'You do take my point!' One imagines a party political broadcast by Mr English. He would hold up a Tory manifesto and say, 'You may care to read paragraph 5, subsection II' then hold up a Green Paper on possible changes to the Allotments and Smallholdings (Scotland) Order 'and compare it to page 17, line 34 of this! You do take my point!'

It is said, with what truth I do not know, that his greatest ambition is to become Speaker. This is a worthy aim, and one can only wish him well. But one should remind him of the old Hispanic phrase: 'No Speaker Da English.'

You can tell a lot about the people who attend party conferences by the way they dress. Hats, for instance, are now so rare at the Tory conference that a sighting indicates that you have spotted some harridan who probably believes in capital punishment in schools to restore a sense of discipline. A battered tweed jacket and a pork pie hat means you have sighted the Earl of Some-place-or-other which Peter Walker did away with in his local government re-organization. Someone in a purple frilly dress shirt with a huge velvet bow tie and cummerbund is undoubtedly a Young Conservative. Someone in an unfrilly purple shirt is Mr Norman St John-Stevas.

Similarly at the Liberals'. Basically the Liberal Party is divided between wispy beards and others. Wispy beards (to be fair, some of them have quite solid growths, like lichen on an ancient monument) wear T-shirts with slogans on, usually faintly dated, e.g. 'The Only Safe Fast Breeder is A Rabbit'. They tend to have ill-fitting jeans, and those heavy shoes which look like Cornish pasties. They have brief-cases stuffed with documents, chiefly about community politics, nuclear power and ecology. They drink real ale. They are suspicious of David Steel. They dislike Tories, *Guardian* reporters, and the other type of Liberal.

The other type of Liberal is often a schoolteacher or small shopkeeper. He can be spotted by his sports coat and grey flannel trousers. He does not have a briefcase, though he is usually clutching a bunch of pamphlets about the things that interest him: site value rating and electoral reform. He is probably a Gilbert and Sullivan fan. He drinks Watney's sparkling keg beer and likes David Steel very much indeed. He is extremely sorry that the Liberals are no longer in a position to keep the Government in power, because this means that the dawn of site value rating and electoral reform is as far away as ever. On the other hand, the wispy beards are, if the truth be told, rather glad. Power does not concern them much. Causes concern them, and they have long learned that causes are seldom advanced by the access of power. Therefore they are happy to lug around their briefcases, and make short, sarcastic remarks to each other, e.g. 'That point of view comes not altogether as a surprise from our friend Roger!' or 'I would hardly have expected the Commission on Land

DAVID STEEL

Tax Reform to have come to a conclusion this side of 1984!'

It is this interest in ideas, rather than power-broking, that makes the Liberals so attractive and, dare one say it, so necessary to British politics. The talk in the Labour conference bars is about block votes and NEC places. The talk at the Liberals' is about nuclear power and site value rating.

There ought to be a word for what I am trying to get at. It's not quite 'seriousness' since that implies a dull, high-minded quality. It isn't 'charisma', which describes a glamour and a mystique which certainly the people I am writing about do not all share. 'Gravitas' might do, except that carries overtones of grey beards and low, slow voices. 'Weight' might pass as shorthand for the concept, but the use of such a word could cause offence to people like Mr Whitelaw and Mr Hattersley – the latter, as it happens, much slimmer than he was. What I am trying to express is an ability to impress your colleagues, a knack of convincing them that you are someone to whom it is worth paying attention, the kind of man of whose remarks people might be heard muttering 'y-e-e-s, that could well be the case,' rather than sniggering behind their hands. In short, it is The Ability To Be Taken Seriously. TATBTS, or just TABS for short.

We can best define TABS by seeing who has got it. Jim Callaghan has got it. Margaret Thatcher has got it, *ex officio* so to speak. David Steel has it, but John Pardoe hasn't. Tony Benn hasn't got it. Nor has Michael Heseltine.

Tony Benn, for instance is taken terribly seriously by the media and also by a lot of people who mistakenly imagine he is a threat to democracy. On the contrary he is the threat *of* democracy. Tony Benn wants to extend democracy into every nook and cranny of our lives, so that we are obliged to take decisions about everything from nuclear waste disposal to the siting of park benches.

Since everyone would be permanently engaged in public debates on the issues of the day, they would have no time for drinking, playing cards or making love. Since no decision about anything could be taken without full public discussion, dictators could arise neither at national nor parish council level.

But Mr Benn is not taken seriously by his colleagues at Westminster. Well, one or two of them perhaps. Mr Brian Sedgemore, before the ungrateful electors of Luton slung him out, used to take Tony Benn seriously for a lot of the time. So did the excellent novelist Mr Joe Ashton (Bassetlaw) who has unaccountably popped up as a Shadow Energy Minister. I suppose Mr Michael Meacher (Oldham West) must take him seriously, at least on weekdays. But I can't, off hand, think of many other MPs.

Similarly, Mr Michael Heseltine. The Tory conference loves Mr Heseltine. They adore the 'axing' of quangos (which as far as one can see involves the sacking of a number of rather able people who often gave their time and advice for little or no payment). Tory MPs regard Mr Heseltine as rather an easy joke. Confident there will never be any nonsense in their party about grass roots supporters electing the leader, they know that Mr Heseltine can have 24-hour standing ovations at Blackpool without it mattering a fig to them. Mr Heseltine is hopelessly lacking in TABS, and there is an end to it.

TABS is transferable. You can be given it, like money or Christmas presents. Norman St John-Stevas didn't have any. Then Margaret Thatcher decided to give him a great big chunk. Then she took it away again. Lord Carrington had oodles of it, almost as much of it as he had money. But Humphrey Atkins is, sadly, rather short. Like clubmen who have run up a few debts, he is a spot strapped for TABS.

David Howell has some but not very much. Sir Geoffrey Howe could use a bit more. Sir Keith Joseph is always running dangerously short.

On the Labour side, Mr Roy Hattersley has had a sudden access of it. His colleagues used to snigger about Mr Hattersley, just as people who were once certified lunatics cannot do anything which does not appear to others mad. Mr Hattersley could not do anything which did not appear to confirm the consuming ambition he was assumed to have. Suddenly, though, his colleagues have started to take him at his own valuation, which is fairly high. He has TABS in plenty now. Dr David Owen is short of it, however, and Mr Roy Mason has very little. The late Anthony Crosland was, and one hesitates to use the phrase of any politican, a fairly brilliant man, beloved of serious journalists and even flippant ones. But he lacked TABS, and so came bottom of the last leadership contest, well below inferior opposition.

All this proves nothing at all, but it might account for the puzzlement people often feel about the difference between what they read in the papers and what actually transpires. 'Why didn't Shirley Williams become leader of the Labour Party?' and 'How did that woman get to be Prime Minister?' they inquire. The answers to these and other questions are diffuse and complicated, but TABS has a lot to do with it.

Cambridge in the thirties appears to have been an open society compared to the Tory party these days. There are so many conspiratorial meetings going on, it is becoming hard for MPs to keep up with them. Secretive left-wingers in the Conservative ranks gathered after dinner in a basement room to discuss their tactics against Mr Whitelaw's plans to exclude the husbands of women who are not born in this country. No sooner had they finished than they had to scurry to another room to discuss how best to force the Government to drop its plans for the so-called 'assisted places', the curious scheme by which intelligent boys and girls can be taken away from perfectly good state schools and forced to face the hideous privations of life in one of our minor public schools.

The 'Fourth Man' in all this, the chap who recruits

idealistic young men to follow their consciences and serve left-wing causes, is Sir Nigel Fisher, MP for Surbiton who chaired the meeting on the new race rules. Even though the Whips know all about Sir Nigel's secret activities, he has been heaped with honours, and has not even been stripped of his knighthood. I cannot imagine that this will last for much longer.

The 'Fourth Man' Anthony Blunt was named by the Prime Minister in the Commons in November 1979.

It is curious to see that the Blunt affair has revealed one of the fundamental truths about British politics, which is that they are organized on class rather than ideological grounds. It is the right-wing and more old-fashioned Conservative MPs who have been quickest to excuse his behaviour. John Stokes, the MP for Halesowen, who is an old-fashioned English gent of right-wing persuasion, appears to believe that the whole thing was got up by the press. Winston Churchill, who is almost as right wing as Stokes, and that is saying a lot, said that we should respect a man who had acted according to his conscience. Meanwhile the Labour left has been pursuing him with the fury normally reserved for monetarists and people who want to increase defence spending.

The fact is, of course, that the Tories instinctively recognize one of their own and the Labour left knows when one of the enemy has strayed into range of their guns. If it had turned out that he had been spying for the Germans,

I suspect that the reactions would have been almost identical.

There is, of course, a long queue of people now claiming to be the first to have identified Blunt. One who can be said to have some justification is Tom Howarth, a Fellow of Magdalene College, Cambridge, who recently wrote a book entitled *Cambridge Between the Wars* in which he described Blunt as a significant Marxist influence at the university in that period. Last Sunday Howarth gave the sermon at the University Church, Great St Mary's. Though it had nothing to do with recent events, it had the intriguing title of 'God's Spies'.

MPs always complain about the Whips in much the same way as schoolboys complain about prefects.

The word is filtering out from the ranks that the Whips' office is not doing quite as brilliantly as, perhaps, it was hoped. There have been a number of mistakes. Mrs Thatcher has not been slow to point them out – even in public. It is argued that with its enormous majority, the Government ought to be rather more successful at organizing the affairs of the House of Commons. The Whips'

50

answer is that it is the very size of the majority which makes their job so hard since MPs feel safe to rebel, knowing the Government will not be defeated. Times have changed. The old Tory Whips' office had two cartoons, a 'Now' one showing the Chief Whip on his knees pleading with MPs who are gliding away to attend 'an urgent dinner party, old boy.' The 'Then' cartoon showed a ferocious, bristle-browed Chief Whip saying to a timid member 'and suppose everybody went swanning off to his wife's funeral!'

Her colleagues began to have doubts about Mrs Thatcher at an early stage.

Further news of Mrs Thatcher. A lot of MPs are getting distinctly rattled by the way she appears to ride roughshod over the Cabinet on almost all occasions. The BBC play about Suez, which depicted a timorous Cabinet tamely agreeing to the frothings of a foolish and dogmatic premier, has given many of them much pause for thought. She has acquired yet another nickname (to go with Attila the Hen, Mrs Mugabe etc) which is the Ayatollah. Not very witty perhaps, but indicative of some deep feeling.

One important occasion when the Cabinet defeated her was over immigration. Mr Whitelaw and most of his colleagues decided that the quota system, which was supposed to slow down the entry of people who have the right to come here, and the register of dependants, were impractical and should be dropped. The register, on which people would have to list the names of children and wives who were not yet here, would have cost many millions of pounds to check and to operate. The Ayatollah insisted that both measures were introduced, but the Cabinet plucked up its courage and overruled her.

Of course this leaves a problem. All the people who voted Tory for various racist reasons, are now likely to

M.T.

feel cheated since the much vaunted immigration controls aren't going to exist. About the only one that is will be the ban on women not born here being allowed to bring in husbands. This is a pointless measure which will lose the Government much residual goodwill in the Asian community while keeping out a total of perhaps no more than 1,000 people a year. But when the Tories drop it they will have virtually no immigration policy left.

Last week the Prime Minister paid a visit to the Department of Employment and was, how can we put it, somewhat tart with the civil servants. One who witnessed it told me, 'It wasn't that she was rude. She just had a highly pointed question for everybody, and then swept on her way almost before they could answer. She doesn't seem to realize that you make twice as bad an impression when you're Prime Minister.'

She must, presumably, have done something to offend Mr John Peyton. The former Minister of Transport was being teased about a gift which the Tory backbenchers gave Mrs Mugabe before the summer recess this year. In a gesture of sycophancy remarkable even for the Tory party, they presented her with a silver brooch as a tribute for the work she had done on their behalf, her splendid qualities of leadership, and so on and so forth. Peyton was being taxed about why he had chipped in towards this grovelling gift. 'It's all right,' he said, 'I only contributed to the pin.'

A massive struggle now looms over the private member's bill to relax the licensing laws. The bill is being introduced by Sir Nicholas Cosmo Bonsor, the Tory MP for Nantwich, who not only sounds like a Sherlock Holmes villain but, with his slanty Chinese eyes, actually looks like one. (My companion reclined in his chair, and placing his fingers together, remarked, 'It is no exaggeration to say, Watson, that Sir Nicholas Cosmo Bonsor is the most fiendishly clever man in Europe.')

Sir Nicholas is also of an extremely right-wing persuasion. He told an American with whom he was eating in White's Club that the two most dangerous men in British politics were Tony Benn and Lord Carrington.

Opposing him is a curious group of teetotallers who have their own committee in the House. This committee, which consists largely of Methodists from all three main parties, is not exactly secret, but it is clandestine. It has been meeting to organize opposition to the Bonsor bill.

One of its leading lights is Mr Ron Lewis, the Labour MP for Carlisle. When the Heath Government decided to sell off the state-owned brewery in Carlisle, Mr Lewis found himself torn between conscience and ideology. He decided in the end that if people were going to drink beer they might as well drink tasty, publicly brewed beer, so he opposed the sale. The brewers sent him a barrel of the stuff down from Carlisle for MPs to taste, but Lewis drew the line at offering the demon barleycorn to his colleagues. Instead it went to the press bar where it was sold off for 3p a pint.

Prime Ministers love summits. One of the things they love most about them, apart from the batteries of television cameras, the delicious food, the murmuring attentions of the officials and the sheer, wonderful, overwhelming sense of self-importance, is meeting famous people.

Prime Ministers are like anybody else. They might know, rationally, that they themselves are famous, but they don't feel it any more than the rest of us do. Meeting famous people is as exciting for them as it would be for us if we went to a party and found, for example, Denis Healey or Richard Baker were among the guests. We wouldn't shut up about it.

'I was chatting to Denis Healey at a party the other day, and he seemed to think that the public sector borrowing requirement was going to go through the roof! His very words!' Or, 'Actually, we got this record of *One Hundred Best-Loved Classical Melodies* because Richard Baker told us it was marvellous.'

Prime Ministers name drop like anyone else. They say things like, 'I made this very point the other day to Jimmy – Jimmy Carter,' or 'Valéry, old chap, I said, you won't get away with this one!' You couldn't shut Harold Wilson up. He was forever hammering on about the famous show business people he knew, all of whom were presumably boasting at the same time about their close acquaintance with Harold Wilson. Perhaps you saw Margaret Thatcher at the rally before the election where those obscure singers and performers joined her on the platform. She positively glowed.

The most famous person there seemed to be Pete Murray. Back in his TV heyday Mrs Thatcher was in her early thirties, and nobody had ever heard of her. Perhaps it is fanciful to imagine that she wore a beehive hairdo and a bouffant skirt as she stood by the jukebox in the coffee bar doing the hand-jive, but she may well have cast a glance at *Six-Five Special* before going out to some political or legal dinner and said to herself, 'Gosh, one day I might

IT'S CALLED POWER-SHARING.
I'LL DROP THE NAMES —
YOU DROP THE BRICKS!!

get to meet Pete Murray!' Not only has she met him now but his wife has written an admiring biography of her.

That is why they enjoy summits so much; it's being seen, on equal terms, with Valéry and Helmut and – well, perhaps the others are not quite so famous. Imagine how thrilled they must be to be rubbing shoulders with her!

Clearly something is affecting her. In Dublin I encountered a BBC reporter who had recently filmed an interview with 'Mrs Mugabe'. As he and the cameraman were making the arrangements, he mentioned that his next assignment was to cover an OPEC meeting. Suddenly she fixed those steely blue eyes upon them.

'If you want to help the British economy,' she said in ringing tones, 'persuade them not to put up the price of oil!' The reporter flinched at this order, distinctly nonplussed. But the cameraman was, on the contrary, entirely plussed. In broad cockney he said, 'All right darlin', I'll do my best!'

The British will never understand Ireland. A colleague on the *Irish Times* recalled being rung up some years ago by the *Daily Mail*. They wanted him to do an interview with Cardinal Conway, who had just become Primate of Ireland. He explained that there was no chance, at that stage, of his getting the interview.

'OK then, interview his wife!' the *Mail* executive shouted back.

Dr Garret FitzGerald, who is Leader of the Opposition in Ireland and one of the half-dozen most intelligent politicians in the British Isles, was, in the mists of time, Dublin correspondent for the *Financial Times*. Some time ago the *FT* needed an article in a hurry about some event that had taken place. Unfortunately, the staff correspondent was away. The order went out to find a former stringer who might be bullied or cajoled into writing the piece, and somebody, riffling through a book of phone numbers, found FitzGerald's name and rang him.

'We need five hundred words by nine o'clock,' he barked down the phone.

'But you don't understand,' FitzGerald replied, 'I'm the Foreign Minister now.' It says something about him that he wrote the article anyway — and phoned it over on time.

One baffling aspect of politics is the way that preferment does not necessarily require talent or ability. In these predictions at Christmas 1979, I was right about some names and entirely wrong about Fowler and Dunwoody.

Around the winter solstice it is the tradition, particularly at the end of a decade, to look forward to the future. In the world of politics we often ask ourselves who will be the names of tomorrow, the people who rest in obscurity now but will soon be household words as much as Thatcher or Healey.

(Conor Cruise O'Brien, to digress a moment, had an ancestor, or at least a distant relation, called Tom Kettle. He was once introduced on a public platform by Parnell, who announced, 'The name Kettle is a household word in Ireland.')

It is just as interesting, though, to look forward and ask ourselves which names, now familiar from their daily appearances on our TV screens and in our newspapers, will, with any luck, be entirely forgotten in ten years. Is it too much to hope that Mr Angus Maude, the Mekon, will be despatched to obscurity by then? Mr Maude has the title Paymaster General, and appears to have some nominal job supervising the Government's publicity. If so, he cannot be doing it very well.

I do not believe that Mr Norman Fowler will still be our Minister of Transport in 1981, never mind 1990. Surely the Social Security Minister, Reg Prentice, will go away to his *dacha*, provided by a grateful government for his defection from the other side. One day he will find the heating cut off, his cheque from the Central Committee will not arrive, friends anxiously inquiring about his welfare will be told that he is on holiday for a long time.

On the Labour side, surely we must be about to hear the end of Fred Mulley, a final snooze in the lobby and the conclusion of a long and undistinguished career. Will David Ennals ever return to the Front Bench? We must hope not.

One day, perhaps, Gwynneth Dunwoody will disappear; the enormous bulk of Mr Arthur Lewis MP will evanesce, and the slighter form of Mr Frank Allaun may dwindle into nothing. Mr Lewis might, in fact, implode like a dying star, and so become a Black Hole, so unimaginably dense that no light can escape from it. If so, how will we be able to tell the difference? What a delight it would be if Mr Nicholas Fairbairn were to climb into a police phone box, the Tardis, and return to the nineteenth century, which he was ill advised ever to leave. Dr Rhodes Boyson might also clamber back into his Cruikshank engraving and return to whichever unpublished Dickens novel he appears in.

Mr Winston Churchill MP revealed that he had had an affair with the notorious Mrs Kharshoggi, alias Sandra Jarvis of Leicester, who became known in the Commons as Mrs Cash and Carry.

Contrary to what some MPs would have you think, I don't believe for one moment that they are all having affairs with the ex-wives of arms dealers, beautiful models, East

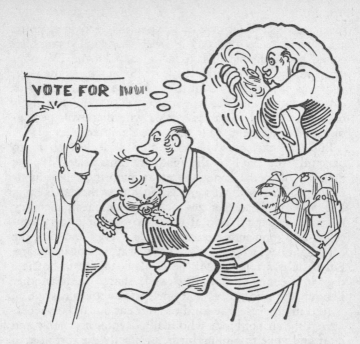

German spies or even off-duty shop assistants. I suspect that this silly rush to claim that they all lead sex lives which would raise Rod Stewart's eyebrows is simply a form of juvenile boasting, like the boring bloke at the office pub who always insists on telling you what he did with the girl from the typing pool.

Naturally a number of MPs do have affairs as, though readers may find this hard to credit, do some of the journalists who are appointed to write about MPs' failings. There is an unwritten code in the Commons which, among other things, means that wives are never told; another article in the same code was invoked the other day when MPs surrounded Winston Churchill, apparently to congratulate him. This code is so strong that some MPs flaunt their mistresses at the Commons without even bothering to pretend that they are secretaries, nieces or the like. One former cabinet minister was so open that people assumed she was his wife; one day an MP accidentally stumbled across his companion's legs in the dark of the TV room and apologized, using the name of the mistress. The wife, who was paying a rare visit to the House, was not pleased. Another junior minister was scarcely ever seen without his mistress. When he introduced his wife there was perceptible embarrassment, as if she were the interloper.

But, and this must be said loud and clear so as to penetrate the skull of the maddest fantasizing MP, the majority of (perhaps not the great majority, but indubitably most) married MPs are as faithful as the day is long. For a start, the exigencies of whipping mean that any intimate dinner for two at the Savoy is liable to be cancelled at a moment's notice. If he is a Tory and rich, the MP might have a handy town flat in, say, Cadogan Square. But if he is a Labour MP he is likely to live in horrible digs in Kennington or Stockwell, shared with another Labour MP who snores and is worried about his sciatica.

And in any case, the kind of man cut out to be a womanizer, the sort of bloke who really devotes his energy and craft and guile to pulling birds, is exactly the sort of man who doesn't become an MP, who spends his life touring round draughty halls, council house estates, and unspeakably boring meetings, all to further his ambitions to rule the rest of us. It is, I am sure, this almost unconscious sense of guilt about having led so boring a life that makes them such lunatic romancers about sex.

I was also quite wrong about Lord Soames's prospects in Zimbabwe.

I am worried about the choice of Lord Soames as Viceroy in Zimbabwe. I do hope that someone has reminded him that times have changed since the days when a hatful of ostrich feathers created whatever effect the gunboat had failed to manage. In particular I hope Lord Soames will not treat the people he has to deal with in the way he treats constituency officials.

For Lord Soames has tried in his time to get innumerable seats and every time he has failed, in spite of his fame, in spite of his mighty rank and in spite of the enthusiastic endorsement of successive Tory leaders.

Shortly after his defeat at Bedford in the 1966 election, the safe Tory seat of Honiton came up. The then Mr Soames was not actually shortlisted, which is hardly surprising since the competition included Peter Thorneycroft, Julian Amery and the man who finally got the seat, Peter Emery. After a good deal of string-tugging by Ted Heath, the local association decided to shortlist Soames after all, and the chairman rang him up to bring him the glad news. The butler answered and undertook to seek his master. A few moments later he returned and said, 'I am afraid Mr Soames is taking his lunch. Will you phone back in half an hour?'

This cavalier manner might not have mattered if the subsequent interview in Honiton had gone differently. Soames was asked if he would be available for constituency functions, if his wife would appear, and whether he would live in the constituency.

'Live, live?' he asked. 'Surely nobody *lives* here?'

A malicious Tory wag has at last found a perfect description for Shirley Summerskill, the former Home Office Minister whose long and gloomy countenance casts all who see her into depression, even if they have just won a large sum on the premium bonds.

'She has a face,' the MP said, 'like a well-kept grave.'

Some people are pathologically unable to make their minds up about anything. Many – perhaps most – MPs suffer from the opposite condition; they are incapable of not having a point of view about everything. Whatever the subject – nuclear power, incomes policy, transport subsidies, who should captain the England cricket team – they know excactly where they stand and they are almost pathetically eager to share their opinion with the rest of us. And the press, about which so many MPs spend so much time complaining, encourages this state of affairs by implying that their views are indeed of great import. This is not enough, however. It could just be that, owing to the Speaker's inexplicable decision not to call some particularly long-winded member, some slip-up in the post which prevented the letters editor of *The Times* from receiving his views on whale conservation, the annoying decision of the US President to resign on the day that his speech on tax reform would otherwise have reached the public print, an MP's views on some subject or other have slipped through this finely-meshed net and have failed to appear in printed form anywhere in the world. At this point the Early Day Motion comes to the rescue.

The EDM, technically a motion for debate as soon as possible, is in fact not going to be debated at all. Perhaps only one in a thousand does get debated, and then only because it fits into some procedural scheme being plotted by the Government. The clue is in the heading to the list of EDMs which appears each week in the Notice Of Motions And Orders Of The Day: 'Notices of motions for which no days have been fixed.' This means motions for which neither Government nor Opposition have made time available and so cannot be debated. Instead they are the undead; or perhaps, like the souls of unborn children, they may be said to exist but have no corporeal reality. Indeed they are not really motions at all, but opinions cast in the form of motions. The heading in the official papers ought to read: 'Opinions Held By Various Windbags Who Could Not Think Of Any Other Way Of Getting Into Print.'

And what a wide selection there are! The latest list of EDMs shows that no fewer than 285 have been tabled in this Parliament alone. Some have attracted only one signature, such as Customs & Excise (SI 1979, No 565) from Mr Harry Ewing. Others, such as Procedural Reform, have been signed by no fewer than 268 people. Some are on mighty subjects such as the Boat People, Peace in the Middle East and Famine in Cambodia, so that one is irresistibly reminded of the old joke about the man who says that his wife makes all the trivial decisions in their house, such as where they go on holiday, when they should move house, whether they need a new car, and he makes all the important ones, such as whether Red China should be admitted to the UN. One often wonders what effect they imagine these motions will have. Would Pol Pot have become a wise and benignant ruler because 131 MPs thought he ought to be?

Other motions are on more parochial topics such as rural transport in the Grampian Region (five signatures) the Upholstered Furniture (Safety) Regulations (eight names) and the Dismissal of Mr Archibald Gilchrist (one). Others hint at festering parliamentary quarrels which have suddenly burst into the open. Mr Denis Canavan and 38 of his colleagues signed A Curt, Evasive Reply. Eight people signed Conduct Of The Honourable Member for Dudley West, the same number who agreed with Mr Frank Hooley (of Sheffield Heeley) on the subject of The Mayor of Nablus. However Sir Frederic Bennett could find only one colleague to support his sternly-titled Abandonment of Double Standards.

Some attract amendments which in turn attract counter-amendments, sometimes going on for days, like a long rally in a tennis match. A Labour motion might 'deplore this disgraceful decision by the Government to allow fifty old people to starve because of expenditure cuts'. A Tory amendment might point out that Labour cut back more money for old people's homes than the new government had. A further Labour amendment adds 'but did not permit anyone to starve as a result.' The Tories answer that, so that in the end the whole motion looks like some lop-sided Christmas tree, festooned with contradictions and garlanded with rebuttals.

Another hopelessly mistaken prediction. . .

I see that the youthful and dynamic Mr Bryan Davies is being tipped as a future General Secretary of the Labour Party. Not a job that anyone in their right mind would want, but then politics does strange things to people. We can be sure, though, that Mr Davies who, until the election was an MP and has bounced back as Secretary of the Parliamentary Labour Party (a quite different job), will show greater qualities of tact and diplomacy if and when he takes over from the rebarbative Ron Hayward.

A year or so ago a colleague and I found ourselves chatting to Mr Davies at a bar in Blackpool. It was during one of many boring sessions at the Labour Party conference. Mr Davies was in an agitated state. His car, he explained, had just been stolen. He had driven it all the way up from London and it had been nicked in Blackpool. We inquired politely what make the car was.

'Make, make?' he said shiftily, 'I don't know what make it is.' We expressed some surprise. Surely the most ignorant owner must know at least roughly what marque his car is. 'I'm simply not interested in that kind of thing,' he replied loftily, as if we were a pair of those peculiar people who can always tell you the wheel configuration on a railway engine or memorize bus timetables. But, we said, the police must have asked him. 'I just told them what it looked like,' he answered.

Even two fuddled hacks realized that something was wrong here, as indeed it proved to be. A little more pressure produced the fact that Mr Davies was the owner of a foreign car, a rather splendid Audi, and was anxious to keep the fact out of the public sheets. Unhappily, his ruse has failed.

Eric Heffer, the MP for Liverpool Walton, has proved one of the column's most popular regular characters.

I have to report, as Mr Walter Annenburg would have said, certain elements of refurbishment at the Commons, in this case refurbishment of Mr Eric Heffer's image. As this column has pointed out before, although Mr Heffer is the mildest and most gently disposed of men, he used to give a ferocious appearance. One imagined him in charge of, for example, a Siberian work camp or one of our minor public schools. Part of the trouble was his spectacles, which were of the type Frankie Howerd used to call 'cruel glasses'. They had very heavy rectangular black frames, and the lenses were set at an angle so that they appeared to be swooping on to his nose, like a buzzard's eyebrows.

Your correspondent often used to warn Mr Heffer about these glasses, and each time he laughed off the warnings. How, he asked, could anyone imagine that he, Eric Heffer, warm hearted, jovial, everybody's pal, was actually a ferocious and uncompromising ideological vopo? Now, I am delighted to report, the glasses have been got rid of and replaced by a much lighter and more graceful pair, of the type favoured by short-sighted hairdressers and French pop singers.

But this is not all. Mr Heffer has been changing his position on the Market, to which he is now not half as opposed as once he was (though not quite as much in favour as he was before that). Watching Mr Heffer move his position on anything is like watching an ocean liner turning 180 degrees to avoid an iceberg. One is impressed by the skill rather than the speed of the operation.

At the same time, Mr Heffer has been one of the most vocal left-wing backbenchers when it comes to speaking out against the Soviet Union. The Left contains some people – and this is not libellous – who are virtually Communists. One such is Joan Maynard (Sheffield Brightside) who is occasionally pictured in the *Morning Star* tossing the odd coconut to open a fund-raising fête. Worse than that, it contains some mealy-mouthed persons who argue that while the suppression of dissidents, the persecution of Jews, the invasion of Afghanistan etc. might be very regrettable, it is the Tories' job to attack them while we get on with hammering the South Africans, the Chileans and Wandsworth Council. Heffer is not one of these. He has always been ready with passionate and well-informed protests about each new Soviet atrocity, whether show-trials, invasions or sham trade unions.

There's no doubt he sees himself as an important man of destiny. He once broke up the Commons with laughter during a resignation speech (he quit as Tony Benn's deputy over the EEC) by announcing solemnly, 'The whole country knows of my deep interest in Italian socialism.' He is a religious man, and it is alleged, unfairly, that he once said, 'Yes, I was a carpenter too.' You can bet that while he read the various newspaper predictions for the Eighties, all of which put Mr Neil Kinnock in the Labour leadership by around 1984, Eric Heffer would have a wry smile on his face in place of the usual beam. There is one burly figure Mr Kinnock will have to get past first.

Here's a tip. When you go to visit your MP, you have to fill in a small green card in the Central Lobby, giving his name, your name and the purpose of the visit. A messenger then beavers off and comes back in 20 minutes or so with the MP, an appointment time, or else the news that your man is not around. If he isn't there, ask for your green card back. If a circle has been drawn on the back, it indicates that the MP is very much present, but does not wish to see you.

Members of the House of Commons gymnasium have the use of a sauna bath. Quite by chance I frequently used to find myself sitting steaming on the wooden benches next to a very right-wing keep-fit enthusiast Tory MP. He used to talk about politics rather like pub bores do; on the assumption that you agreed with everything he said.

'About time we brought back corporal punishment in primary schools, what say you?' he would ask. Or 'In my view, your average black chap would be a lot happier back where he came from, am I right?' Much later I met him in the Harcourt Room, an undistinguished and overpriced dining place in the Commons where MPs can take guests. There is a small bar there for people who are waiting for their table to be ready. The MP was entertaining some constituents.

'Ah!' he exclaimed as I passed, 'I'd like to introduce you to. . .' The last thing I wanted before dinner was a chat with people who thought like him, and suddenly I knew what I had to say. I stared blankly at him for a moment, then said: 'Sorry, old chap, but I didn't recognize you with your clothes on.'

As I chewed my under-ripe avocado I could still hear him explaining in embarrassed tones just what I actually must have meant.

Once again, Britain's civil servants are under attack for not doing what they are told by the politicians.

Disgraceful, many people will say. It is quite clear that most politicians are, if not quite round the twist, at least not fully twenty shillings to the pound. How fortunate we are to have a keen, alert Civil Service to guard against the worst excesses of the politicians and to guide them, gently but surely, like a blind man across a road.

I fear that this is a naive point of view. In my admittedly limited experience, if there is one class of person who knows even less than a politician it is a civil servant. At least politicians occasionally have to make sporadic contact with reality like the crew of the Starship Enterprise being beamed down to an unfamiliar planet. Sometimes they are obliged to visit a working men's club, or a sale of work, or the site of some factory which is about to close down. Civil servants do none of this. The only members of the public they meet are other civil servants on the train home to East Croydon, unless a member of the working class chances to join their madrigal singing society.

I have been asking various cabinet ministers, present and past, about their experience of civil servants. Most of them, it must be said, speak highly of the ones they know personally. But all of them have some story about how the Civil Service manipulates its so-called masters. One told me: 'Their favourite trick is using your daily schedule. You are attending a meeting, and they know you are likely to take a decision they won't like. But they also know you have an even more important meeting an hour later. So, almost without you realizing, they spin the first one out until there is no time for the important discussion. That means you have to take their word for it, and rubber-stamp what they want – unless you are extra careful.'

Another said that if they don't like the conclusion of a cabinet paper the minister has asked them to draw up, they might put in one or two deliberate mistakes. They will then ring up their opposite number in another ministry to tip him off. 'So the other man tells his minister what the fault in the paper is, and it can be destroyed in Cabinet. Your man is trounced and humiliated. When he complains, the civil servants simply apologize and promise it won't happen again.'

It is good to see that Mr Gerry Fitt, the splendid Catholic MP for West Belfast, has lost none of his wit. Being on the receiving end of a Fitt barb must be like getting a mortar in your stomach. Recently the tiny Belfast MP Johnny McQuade, who is a member of Ian Paisley's Democratic Unionist Party and who makes the good doctor sound like a faint-hearted liberal, was boasting about his days in the Chindits. He had, he said, parachuted no fewer than 23 times behind Japanese lines.

'What a pity,' Fitt remarked, 'that you kept landing on your head.'

The word 'Lobby' has a multitude of parliamentary meanings. It refers to the 100 or so journalists with access to the corridors of power, to the three separate chambers or vaults – Members' Lobby, Central Lobby and Lords Lobby – which are joined together in line and form the central nervous system of the Palace of Westminster, and it also refers to the practice of a large group of people arriving in the place in order to buttonhole their MP and belabour him with their views.

These groups tend to be massed in the Central Lobby, an area roughly the size of St Paul's, which manages to be simultaneously vast and claustrophobic, so weighty is the press of over-decoration. The floor resembles a refugees' transit camp, or how one imagines a passport office in the Soviet Union. As knots of people wait for their MP to be dragged unwillingly from the discreet warmth of the Chamber, the Strangers' Bar or the Terrace Tea Room, a policeman reads out the names of the lucky suppliants over a loudspeaker. In its journey across the Lobby from the policeman's microphone, the name rebounds several times from the walls, the gilded frescoes and the richly patterned tiling, so that by the time it reaches its intended hearer it has been reduced to a dull low-pitched booming noise, like the mysterious sound in Forster's Marabar Caves. Frequently an MP with a hunted expression can be seen at the policeman's elbow as he calls for 'Mr Ommmmm'. Mr Pettigrew, not recognizing this as his own name, is unaware that his MP has turned up and, after a brief wait, the MP is able to skulk back to resume his study of Japanese porcelain imports or a large scotch.

A while ago the Lobby was packed, entirely jammed, with supporters of the campaign against the Corrie Abortion Bill. Many had babies, which they clutched to their fronts instead of their backs, like dyslexic Indian squaws. Members of Dutch Women Against Corrie (how did they get there?) chatted to the International Contraception, Abortion and Sterilization Campaign, which seems to have got most eventualities covered.

One or two were wearing plastic construction helmets

with stickers saying 'Save Our Steel'. Were they the militant wing, anti-SDP Liberals, or had they merely strayed into the wrong lobby? It turned out that they were in the right place, and were making a political point about a general assault on the working class. There were dozens of side-lobbies, performances by The Brighton Theatre Against Sexism, meetings of the Nurses For the Right To Choose. There were pictures of dripping knitting needles intended – and succeeding – in showing the horrors of self-abortion. Somebody was carrying round a five-foot wire and paper coat-hanger designed to make the same point.

Into this seething vivarium the occasional MP would step gingerly. Some were bolder, perhaps because of their record against the bill. Others had that air of peculiar trepidation as one who is terrified but determined not to show it, like a middle-aged man asking a group of skinheads the way to a church fête. Those who did not please were discussed with scorn at small informal gatherings afterwards. 'He thought Clause 1 was the most important!' or 'He thought the charities were making fortunes out of counselling!' It is a curious phenomenon that when a bill, like this one, excites immense public interest, the voters often know far more about the details of the legislation than the MPs. No wonder most of our representatives heartily wish that the whole issue would pack up and go away for ever. Whatever the fate of the Corrie bill this month, we can be sure that will not happen.

It was, incidentally, in the Central Lobby, Mrs Kharshoggi informed us through the pages of the *Daily Star*, that she first set eyes on, and fell in love with, Mr Winston Churchill. Presumably this was not during a mass lobbying, or else they could not have set eyes on any part of each other, never mind fallen in love. I hear that a number of MP's wives decided to throw a scare into their (possibly) errant husbands by leaving embarrassing messages for them. They would ring the Commons number (01–219 3000, if you feel like a good moan to your MP) and ask for the husband. If he was not available, they would leave a message saying that Mrs Kharshoggi had called. When one or two wives discovered that the attendants would take down the message and pass it on, several others used this method to win a small but pleasing revenge for their husband's absence.

Not long ago a small group of Tories found themselves supping with Mrs Thatcher, and raised the question of child benefit, the new family allowance which is paid to the mother. They were astonished to hear her say that she was opposed to the whole principle of the benefit, on the grounds that it was not given to the head of the household.

'I believe that it weakens the family,' she said firmly. Does she really hand over her entire pay packet to Denis every month? One finds this hard to believe.

Denis put in a surprising appearance the other day at a meeting Mrs Mugabe held with senior civil servants in Downing Street. They had been admitted through the famous front door (Number 10 is really just a luxurious office-block with a sort of penthouse for the PM on top) and were met by the lady. She pointed to a door and urged them to enter, saying she would follow in a few moments.

The civil servants knocked softly at the portal, and, hearing no reply, walked in. There, to their considerable surprise, they saw a couch and on the couch the somnolent – indeed snoring – form of Denis Thatcher. They gently closed the door and waited outside. When she arrived a few moments later she asked, 'Why are you waiting? I told you to go in,' and in they went. She observed the figure on the divan, said nothing at all, and began the meeting. Towards the end he awoke, and stretching himself asked, 'What's been going on?'

'You were asleep,' was his wife's crisp and incontrovertible reply. Nothing more was said, and the civil servants, slightly uncomfortable, left the room.

Mr Dickens, when not attending thés dansants, found ample time to attract columnar attention.

More news of Mr Geoffrey Dickens, the new Huddersfield MP who ostensibly sits in the Conservative interest, but in fact votes Labour or abstains whenever he has the chance. He rapidly neared the stage of hand-to-hand combat with Mr Spencer Le Marchant, the admirable Tory Whip with the wretched job of attempting to persuade Mr Dickens, just now and again, to go into the same division lobby as the rest of his party.

On the rare occasions that he does, and Mr Le Marchant is a teller, it is his practice to count thus: '84...85... 86...87..*so* good of you to join us tonight, Mr Dickens ...88...89.' He has, less politely, adopted a four letter epithet beginning with 'c' for Mr Dickens, which he loses no opportunity to employ in his presence.

Not long ago Mr Dickens felt it necessary to talk to the Chief Whip, Mr Michael Jopling. He had heard, he explained, that when a Tory MP could not vote for the Government he had to inform the said Chief Whip. He himself, he said, could not vote on the following occasions because of pressing constituency engagements. No, no, Mr Jopling said, those don't count. If it's a three-line Whip, short of imminent death, you have got to be there. The only excuse for not voting with the Government is a severe attack of conscience. Mr Dickens got angry.

'The trouble wi't thee,' he said, 'is tha' can't understand Yorkshire fowk!' Mr Jopling, who was born and bred in the county, found that he had nothing at all to say.

The success of the 'Dear Bill' column in Private Eye, *led to greater interest in the original.*

Proof at last has come my way to show that Mrs Thatcher's cash limits are really beginning to bite, indeed quite literally to hit home. Cash limits are the system by which a department or a nationalized industry is given a certain amount of money each year, and if it overspends, tough cheddar. A well-known Tory MP, who told me this story, found himself buying smokers' requisites in a small tobacconist's in Whitehall, just opposite Downing Street. The shop is run by two lovable old Cockney ladies, who are something of celebrities round there.

As he waited the familiar figure of Denis Thatcher walked into the shop. He bought 20 Gold Leaf and left the shop. The two old ladies then conversed as follows:

'Did you see who that was?'

'No, who was it?'

''Im from across the road.'

'Did he buy his usual then?'

'Yer, he did.'

'You'd wonder why she doesn't give him enough for 40 so he wouldn't have to come in every day, wouldn't you?'

Another Tory MP tells me that he has found a means of coping with Denis's wife. Her technique, when she talks to anybody on subjects such as the public sector borrowing requirement or cushion cover designs, is to fix them with her blue and piercing glance. This so unsettles them that they are quite unable to marshal any arguments they might presume to have against her. This MP says that he has started staring straight back into those laser eyes. 'One of you has to win, and if you keep it up long enough, it's bound to be you,' he says.

One has to admire Mr Whitelaw, if for no other reason than that his unflappable social manner remains the same for all classes of society, from viscounts to vagrants. As Home Secretary he visited Dartmoor prison, and was taken to see one of the maximum security sections of the gaol. Here the prisoners are kept alone behind thick bars. Willie assumed that he would merely have to examine the captives through the bars, but the Governor had different ideas. He stopped at a cell occupied by a huge black man, about 6' 5" tall. This man was thought so dangerous and unstable that he was stark naked – without even a pair of socks which he might use to hang himself. The Governor smoothly unlocked the door and swung it open.

'This is the Home Secretary,' he said, by way of introduction. The prisoner drew himself up to full height then suddenly advanced on Willie who, though a large man, was a mere midget compared to his new acquaintance.

'I've written to you!' the prisoner roared. Far from being nonplussed, Willie was entirely plussed.

'Excellent. Very good. Delighted to hear it. Quite right, perfectly correct. Very pleased to have met you,' he said, then slammed the cell door shut and fled. The point is that

74

Wm. Whitelaw CH. MC. DL.

he would almost certainly have said exactly the same if it had been the Queen Mother who had addressed him.

Congratulations to Mr Roy Hattersley for equal imperturbability under fire. Asked to a local radio studio to comment on some recent decision by his Tory opposite number Michael Heseltine, he was confronted by a nervous interviewer.

'Er, I wonder if I could ask you, Mr Heseltine. . .' the youth began.

Hattersley leaned forward.

'The name,' he said, 'is Hattersley. I'm the *natural* blond.'

The column's predictions have been erratic, to say the least, but it has had some scoop nicknames.

Backbench Tories have now formally relinquished the name Mrs Mugabe for their leader. They say that it has connotations of moderation, reasonableness and a desire to conciliate which they cannot identify in her. Instead she has become 'Heather', which, they say, denotes a kind of genteel brutality. One of them told me the other day that she reminded him of the banners and placards which used to greet the famous and truculent Leeds defender Norman Hunter. 'Norman Bites Your Leg,' they said.

Quite.

The onset of Lent means that literally dozens of MPs, Tories for the most part, forsake alcohol until Easter.

They make a piteous sight in the Commons bars.

Though they have taken the temporary pledge (most of them, being unversed in the scriptures, do not realize that you do not have to abstain on holy days from whatever it is you have decided to abstain from) they cannot bear to leave the cosy warmth and cheery company of Annie's Bar, the Strangers' and the Smoking Room. Some drink ginger beer, others try orange, grapefruit or tomato juice, some favour bitter lemon, various kinds of sparkling mineral water, or sample something which used to be called the Strawberry Blonde and is nowadays known as the Iron Lady. This is a slimline tonic water with a dash of bitters, so that it looks a little like the traditional naval pink gin. Like most slimline drinks it has a taste which lingers on the palate, so that after a couple of them you feel as if you have been sucking old pennies.

The point about non-alcoholic drinks is, of course, that you cannot drink them one after another like scotch or halves of bitter. Nevertheless the social camaraderie of the bar demands that you do. MPs who have given up for Lent can be easily spotted in the lobbies and refectories of the House by their continuous burping and the lack of appetite induced by the sweetness contained in a dozen Pepsi-Colas. If somebody managed to invent a soft drink which did not taste repulsive after the third glass, he would earn a fortune in the Commons alone.

Mr Denis Healey is the opposite of Mr Attlee, of whom Churchill said in a famous remark that he was a modest man who had much to be modest about. Healey is a pretty vain man, who has a lot to be pretty vain about. Last Saturday he appeared on television debating with the tiny pundit from Chicago, Professor Milton Friedman. After the programme had been recorded Friedman remarked that Healey was the most intelligent man he had encountered in the West.

'You're right,' Healey replied.

Heather's habit of announcing policy off the top of her

Denis Winston HEALEY

head at the Despatch Box is proving wearing on some of her ministers. I met one just before Prime Minister's Questions the other day.

'Can't stop,' he called over his shoulder. 'I have to go in to find out what my next policy is.'

A choice new Willieism:

Speaking on the subject of Britain's overcrowded prisons at a Conservative meeting in Bournemouth the other day, he announced from the platform, 'I don't blame anyone, except perhaps, all of us.'

One of the most delightful characteristics of many politicians is their unselfconscious vanity. This was displayed in iridescent glory during the 1980 Labour leadership campaign.

Is there nobody in the Labour Party who does not see himself as a candidate for the leadership? My list of people who fancy their chances is already a dozen long and there may be others to add. Some of the candidates are fairly obvious, such as Denis Healey and Michael Foot, others less so, such as Roy Mason and Stanley Orme. It is getting to the state now that one might drift into the new Labour HQ in South London, and as one deftly tossed one's cloth cap on to the hat rack, quip lightly to the doorman, 'Well, Albert, standing for the leadership then?' Albert would

79

reply gravely, 'Well sir, a number of people have approached me to inquire what my intentions might be. . .'

Destiny beckons to nobody more menacingly than to Mr Eric Heffer, the Labour MP for Liverpool Walton. Mr Heffer has been going round saying that if Mr Callaghan declines to resign the leadership in November this year, then it will be incumbent on him, as his duty to party and nation, to stand against the former premier. And Mr Heffer has powerful backers. The other week he wrote an article attacking Professor Milton Friedman in *The Times*. A day or so later he received a letter from the Ritz Hotel, saying that it was rare for the sender to read anything he wished he had written himself, but Mr Heffer's article was such an instance. The signature was illegible, but masterly code-cracking work around the bar revealed it to be that of Professor J. K. Galbraith. Getting a letter from Galbraith praising your Keynsian economics is a bit like getting a letter from M. Claude Lévi-Strauss congratulating you on your structural anthropology, or from Mrs Barbara Woodhouse saying how well your dog does its Number Twos. It is praise of a high order.

However, things have not always gone so smoothly for Mr Heffer, who sees himself as the natural predecessor of Mr Tony Benn. I recall a march and meeting in Accrington, against unemployment, organized by the local Labour MP, the dapper and silvery-haired Mr Arthur Davidson. (Mr Davidson has recently changed his hairstyle to pudding-basin, but clearly very expensive pudding-basin. Perhaps it ought to be called Zabaglione-basin.) Mr Heffer wound up the meeting in Accrington Town Hall with a splendid, emotional speech which had the demonstrators standing, clapping and cheering as he finished.

Justly delighted with his success, he set off down the magnificent baronial stairway of the Town Hall. At the bottom was a small man, a sort of Northern millworker as drawn by Giles or Bill Tidy. He had a cloth cap, a muffler, and a long raincoat down to his ankles. Diffidently he approached Mr Davidson.

'Ah wonder if ah might 'ave a word wi' Mr Heffer,' he inquired nervously, twisting his cloth cap in his hands as he spoke.

'But of course,' Mr Davidson replied, then fetched the mighty Heffer figure over. Eric moved towards the little man, clearly expecting ringing praise for his speech, something on the lines of 'Ah once heard Keir Hardie, but he had nowt on thee' perhaps. Instead the small man looked politely up and said, 'Mr Heffer, thou art nothing but a trouble-maker!' turned on his heel, and shuffled quietly away.

I never stop being astonished by what some constituents expect from their MPs. Take this letter, received by Mr Frank McElhone, the Labour MP for Glasgow Queen's Park. A constituent wrote to say that he was paying a visit to London and he would be grateful if Mr McElhone would arrange a ticket for the Strangers' Gallery so that he could watch Parliament at work. The letter went on: 'While preferring to meet you yourself, Frank, I know this is not always possible; so, if you can leave a word with the police in the Central Lobby and a fiver for a drink in Annie's Bar, I'll be more than grateful, Frank.'

As who wouldn't be? Apart from the fact that if he extended the same generosity to all his constituents, it would cost Mr McElhone some £172,000 (and his seat, for bribery), there is the extraordinary Scottish assumption that 'a drink' costs a fiver. Even in London's ghastly and overpriced West End there are places where you can still get half a dozen drinks for that.

Speaking of drink, I have had cause before to warm of the menacing antics of the secret committee of MPs which is devoted to doing away with alcohol. Their latest sinister plan may, with luck, backfire. Mr Tristan Garel-Jones of Watford, and Mr Frank Hooley of Heeley (or perhaps the other way round) have written to the Chancellor asking him to take all forms of drink off the Retail Price Index and have it classified as a drug instead. But even with prescription charges going up to £1, booze would still be remarkable value. 'You're a bit run-down old man, but nothing a case of Hennessy XSOP won't put right. Just take this form round to the off-licence. . .'

It is heartening to report that Mr Harold Macmillan is as sharp in the tooth as ever. His admiration for Mrs Thatcher is generally known to be less than whole hearted. The problem is that in the Conservative Party you are not allowed to say such a thing outright. You require a form of words which can then be translated by your listeners. It's a bit like giving the after-dinner speech at a convention of Morse Code operators; visitors and waiters will not understand your best barbs. For instance, if a Tory wishes to say that the Government is going to hell in a handcart, he must say something on the lines of 'I bow to no one in my admiration for our Prime Minister and the many achievements by her and her team of ministers. It is because I know Mrs Thatcher to be an eminently humane and compassionate politician as well as a practical realist that I am sure she will reconsider the tight money policy which has been doubtless forced upon her . . .' etc. etc. Mr Macmillan is a past master at this kind of talk, which always brings pleasure to his many listeners.

Recently he was elevated from the honorary position of Chairman of the Carlton Club to the even more honorary position of President. His speech turned out to be a heavily ciphered, yet elegant attack on Mrs Thatcher and her monetarist policies. Reading with painful slowness, and with that curious habit of bringing a bit of paper to within half an inch of his eyes when he wants to be sure of something, he talked about the time when 2 per cent inflation was thought dangerous.

'We had to keep inflation down, didn't we, Lord Thorneycroft?' he said, turning to the elderly Chairman of the Tory Party who was also present. (Translation: 'You were a fool to resign over a lousy £50 millions Government overspending, as recent events have proved.')

'We must no more be the slaves of professors than the slaves of dogmas,' he went on, which is code for 'That woman is following some loony Professor, Friedburg or Friedman or something, no wonder everything is going wrong.' He harked back to the golden days of his own administration – 'but that was before the pound began to float and the Cabinet began to leak. . .' i.e. 'Before everybody realized that we were going completely round the bend and might as well jump in the lake now. Nobody leaked from my Cabinets because my policies were so wise and good.'

And so on and so forth. If he had said what he meant bluntly, his listeners would have been shocked and indignant. Since he said it in the accepted Tory Party code, they were delighted.

I've just come back from a visit to the Labour Party's new headquarters, and a very dazzling place it is too. Unlike the old Transport House, which was all gloomy corridors, fading lino and the unmistakable smell of Mansion Polish, the new place looks like a particularly expensive gentlemen's club tarted up by an American advertising agency. There are lush brass and gilt fitments everywhere, marbled fireplaces, mock candelabras hanging from the ceiling and carpets everywhere – so much that they even have deep-pile for the computers to stand on.

Naturally, it is important that in the midst of this luxury, the comrades retain a folk-memory of their roots. There are paintings and drawings of famous Labour figures on all the walls, and in the main boardroom, as used by the National Executive Committee, there is a huge nude male statue, life-sized, entitled *Labour's Awakening*. It's not a very good statue, and would be better entitled *Labour Dropping Off*. It has all the right parts, though, and has been arranged against the wall so as not to offend Miss Joan Maynard, Mrs Renee Short, Mrs Shirley Williams and other female members of the NEC. Actually it does have some bits missing; in its recent travels (it was originally a gift – presumably an ill-will gift – from the National Union of Railwaymen) the statue has lost its toes, which lie forlornly on the bottom of its glass case, like the Venus de Milo with gangrene.

There is, surprisingly, a computer room, which feels a little out of place, like a working men's club built into Conservative Central Office. The computer hums and winks at its operators as it handles wages, sales and purchases. Some of the brighter researchers are trying to programme it to write Shadow Cabinet speeches, though this might be thought wasteful of such a clever piece of machinery.

In the loading bay under the building there are dozens of cases marked 'Tanqueray English Gin'. Regrettably these contain nothing but several thousand copies of out-of-date Labour party reports. But there are thousands upon thousands of beer mats with the famous rude cartoon of Mrs Thatcher on. Four times a day a minibus leaves for the House of Commons. Sometimes it takes nothing but a few copies of the latest illegible speech by Mr Eric Heffer. On one occasion it came back with half the Shadow Cabinet, Mr Healey, Mr Foot and so forth, all ready for a tour of inspection.

The outside of the building is a magnificent Georgian façade. It has no nameplate, presumably for fear of attack from marauding Conservatives, so postmen cannot believe it is the Labour Party. They drop mail at the much grottier Herbert Morrison House just down the road, where they assume the party must live.

I see the most famous George Brown story is doing the rounds again. I suspect that this yarn is one of those 'modern myths' – tales which are passed about by word of mouth, and which are always told as if they were perfectly true. Indeed the teller invariably believes that they are true, and I have heard this story several times from people one would not have thought credulous – Ted Heath for one. The story varies in its details; I have heard it set in Venezuela, France and Carlton House, London, and the punch-line changes, but the main structure is always the same.

The basic version is that George Brown, while Foreign Secretary, attended a banquet and got very drunk. After the meal a band struck up and Brown assumed that dancing was about to begin. Thinking that as the guest of honour he should institute it, he marched unsteadily up to the most ravishing looking creature in the room and said, 'Beautiful lady in red, will you waltz with me?' To this he got the reply: 'No I will not, and for three reasons. First, because you are disgustingly drunk. Secondly, because this is not a waltz but the Venezuelan national anthem. Thirdly, because I am not a beautiful lady in red, but the Papal Nuncio.'

I don't believe the story for one moment, and would challenge anyone to find an eye-witness. But it would be fascinating to learn its origins. Was it a wild exaggeration of some genuine incident in which Brown mistook a Vatican emissary for a woman? Or has the same story been told of all politicians with a penchant for drink over the past 200 years?

I sometimes wonder if the member for Down, South, enjoys being thought a trifle odd.

Enoch Powell's relationship with the real world has always puzzled me. All his ideas, and hence all his speeches and writings, spring from such abstract and academic roots that it is little wonder they bear so distant a relationship to the country and the society in which the rest of us exist. I've never thought of him as an evil racist, although quite a lot of evil racists must have drawn strength and support from what he has said. His speeches on the subject of race relations derive from an old-fashioned romantic nationalism, and not from any evident knowledge of the way black

85

people and white people live, or fail to live, together. His ideas and writings remind me of a barrage balloon that has cut adrift from its moorings, and now floats over the country out of control, bumping into trees, and waiting for some Act of God to puncture it and sent it flabbily to earth.

Yet he can have a sharp interest in popular culture, often quite unexpected. Years ago I saw him in a TV hospitality room. He was about to be interviewed on the decision to vote Labour in the General Election. Another guest on the same programme was Bill Haley, the aged rock'n'roller. Haley was wearing the most extraordinary multi-coloured jacket in two dozen different hues. He looked like a badly-adjusted colour TV.

A nervous researcher suddenly found he had to introduce them, which he effected in a strangulated sort of way.

'Pleased to meet you, Mr Pole,' said Haley, who plainly had no idea who his new friend was.

'And I am pleased to meet *you*,' said Enoch. 'I have always *wanted* to meet you.' I often wondered why. Was Enoch once a secret rocker, with crêpe soles and a string tie?

Not long ago, I learn, Mr and Mrs Powell were guests at a friend's house in Sussex. On Saturday evening the company decided to watch *Dallas* which Enoch had not seen before. It was a fascinating and informative cultural experience for him, and he kept up a running commentary on J.R., Sue-Ellen and so on. At one point he said in surprise: 'Why is that man wearing his hat inside the house?'

'Because he's a Texan, dear,' Mrs Powell said crisply. This answer seemed to satisfy him.

It is fair, I think, to say that most politicians mistrust holidays deeply.

What they mistrust is the way that the country appears to function in a perfectly satisfactory manner in their absence. If, for instance, as we are told, Cabinet meetings are of vital importance every week, how is it that we are spared the threat of nuclear war, doubled inflation and collapse of the Green Pound while the Cabinet takes its customary two or three months' break? There can be few professions, apart perhaps from those of pimps, seal cullers and writers, whose absence is so slightly noticed and so little regretted.

Nevertheless, go away they do – at least most of them. Mr Michael English, the Labour MP for Nottingham West and the only permanent fixture in Annie's Bar apart from the beer pumps, likes to vacation in the Strangers' Bar, Annie's being closed for the summer. Some years ago a colleague went on a walking tour of the Lake District, and, going into a cosy pub and looking forward to a quiet pint, saw to his utter astonishment the ineffable English waiting in the corner of the Snug, all ready to regale him with news about the Select Committee on Public Expenditure. Those who have studied these things say that this is the only recorded instance of English going away for his holidays.

Rich MPs naturally go on rich men's holidays. Some, like Mr Jonathan Aitken, have rich friends dotted all over the globe, and can drop in on their villas as the rest of us might sleep on a friend's couch. Mr Eric Heffer, the lovable yet glowering challenger for Jim Callaghan's position, likes to take his charming wife Doris to the Italian coast, where he is able at first hand to study the problems of Socialism in a declining economy.

Other Labour MPs pride themselves on joining the *hoi polloi* on package tours. The late Tom Litterick, who sat for Selly Oak in the last Parliament, chose to take his young lady on a tour of Crete while some crucial vote was coming in the Commons: he had, he said, left word of his whereabouts with his agent, though it is surprising that the Whips, those most resourceful of men, did not locate him over several days. They even went to the lengths of having a message flashed on to cinema screens on the island – as if somebody would go on holiday to such a place and spend their time watching films in Greek.

Last year Mrs Thatcher made the mistake of going to the Island of Islay, where she had been invited by the chap who owns the place, her loyal backbencher Charles Morrison. The trip was, by all accounts, a disaster. It wasn't that the Morrisons were not hospitable – indeed, they were the epitome of all that is gracious. The fault was really in the clash between two strains of the Tory party: the landed, tweeded gentry, fishin', huntin' and lookin' after the workin' classes, and the entrepreneurial, meritocratic, lettin' the workers look after themselves class, of whom our Prime Minister is the acknowledged leader. So while her hosts were engaged in bucolic Caledonian pursuits, Heather was anxiously tripping off to the teleprinter installed in the house, fretting about the money supply, Zimbabwe and so forth, and generally governing us. This was a mistake. As Harold Macmillan well knew, government has no more need to continue uninterrupted than school-teaching or the ice hockey season.

Mr Callaghan takes modest holidays – he has been perfectly happy in Ireland in spite of the terrorism. Perhaps he thinks that his Irish ancestry – his father's name was Garrigan and this almost cost him his nomination in Cardiff – will see him all right.

A year or so ago, Mr Denis Healey visited Scotland with his wife, Edna. In some far-flung Highland port they were queueing for a ferry when an aged Scottish loon approached them. 'Ha!' exclaimed the aged loon, 'I told me wife that if she didna fill in the VAT returns ye'd be up here after her. And here ye are.'

I see Mrs Thatcher has been going on her famous walkabouts again. This odd term was first used of the Queen during a tour of Australia some years ago, and it refers to an old aborigine custom of a chap wandering off alone into the bush for a few weeks in order to discover himself, kangaroos, and whatever else might be there. In other words, it is more or less the opposite of the walkabout as practised by western politicians, who discover almost nothing in their travels.

Of course that is not the way they see it. Frequently they regard it as a valuable opportunity to find out what is on the minds of the people. Politicians who are famous enough to go on walkabouts – i.e. famous enough to be recognized – tend to be surrounded most of the time by civil servants, sycophantic junior MPs and the grovelling bag-carriers known as 'special advisers'. Having convinced themselves that occasional visits to the Labour Club or to the floor of some soft toy factory in their constituency represents learning how the populace thinks, their only contact with reality is frequently in the shape of their housekeepers or the man who comes over to iron the croquet lawn. So the walkabout, with its endless succession of half-heard questions and garbled answers assumes a significance utterly out of proportion to any value it might have.

Ted Heath populated his speeches with an entire stage army drawn from his walkabouts. There was a docker he had met in Felixstowe, who had assured him that dockers opposed the nationalization of ports, a pensioner he met in (I think) Luton, who was grateful for all the Tories had done for the old folk, even a restaurateur he had met in Shanghai. This last figure, whom I always pictured with a slant-eyed grin and a moustache like Wyatt Earp's necktie, was invoked when Mr Heath was asked about nationalization. He had enquired about a row of cafés, and who owned them, and the restaurateur had explained that they all belonged to the State, but were operated by different individuals. Heath had then visited one and had enjoyed an excellent meal. I always thought this an argument in favour of nationalization, but the audiences didn't seem to notice.

You would imagine, would you not, that before plunging into a seething mass of people, a politician would have prepared a few stock questions or remarks, at least to prevent embarrassment. But of course, because they see the walkabout as such a valuable monitor of the public pulse, they never do this, trusting to the native spontaneity of the electorate. However, the average member of the voting public, suddenly coming face to face with, say, the Leader of the Opposition is immediately tongue-tied. Indeed it's a fair bet that if he isn't struck mute, it's because he is a pretty weird and untypical individual. So the pols are reduced to adlibbing sentiments of quite staggering vapidity. During the last election, Mrs Thatcher marched into a shopping centre in Coalville, Leicestershire, and addressed herself to a young woman in a green horizontal striped jersey. 'What club is that?' she inquired firmly, evidently thinking the girl played rugby in her spare time. The girl stared back open-mouthed and finally managed to say, 'What do you mean?' Mrs Thatcher smiled sweetly back and said, 'I asked what club it was!' She might as well have asked what part of the moon the girl came from.

Another woman was wearing an orange sweater. 'Do you know,' the Leader of the Opposition said, with every appearance of interest, 'the curtains in our bus are exactly that colour?'

Similar staggering coincidences (Arthur Koestler would be fascinated) are part of the stock-in-trade of walkabouts, since they convince the pol that he has a real and genuine link with the people instead of with the pols who normally surround him. Thus, on some factory walkabout, Mr Denis Healey learned that one woman in the canteen was in the habit of holidaying in Ross-on-Wye. It turned out that his wife's mother came from this same borough, and that she had earned her pin money by singing in a local cinema where her accompanist was, wait for it, Jimmy Young's mother. Even this stupendous example of the universal laws of chance failed to win the seat for Labour.

Mr Whitelaw shakes as many hands as he can inside a given minute saying 'How marvellous to see you, how good to meet you!' and moves on at top speed before the people attached to the hands can get a question in. Sir Keith Joseph has the opposite approach; he asks people if they have anything to ask him. Naturally, being completely unprepared for a meeting with Sir Keith Joseph, they never have. Mr Michael Foot stands around, shifting his weight nervously from one foot to the other, and saying 'ha!' and 'well!' until people realize he is shyer than they are, and, in kindly tones, address encouraging remarks to him.

Perhaps inevitably my favourite embarrassing moment from a walkabout was by grace of Ted Heath. This was really a crawlabout – his agent used to pop him into half a dozen pubs in his Bexley-Sidcup constituency and hope that he could summon up the courage to address the drinking public. I felt great sympathy for him; people who can happily address the House of Commons on a crucial confidence motion, or 25 million people on televison, are often seized by crippling shyness when it comes to meeting one perfect stranger. In one pub Heath composed himself, then walked over to the bar where a man was giving his order. The Prime Minister (as he then was) tapped the customer on the shoulder.

The man spun round and saw to his utter astonishment the beaming face of the silvery-haired statesman. Heath beamed a moment longer, then said 'Do you come here often?' The man gargled something in reply, and fled.

Before the police moved me on for loitering, I was able to conduct an in-depth investigation last week on a crucial test of democratic principle. It involves ministerial cars which, for the most part, are sparkling clean, deep-pile carpet-fitted Rover 3.5s finished in a natty chocolate colour which you don't normally see in the sale rooms. In the back there are armrests the size of writing desks, and little adjustable lamps by which ministers can read private papers or, in the case of one member of the last Government, see which end of the whisky bottle to open. They are driven by capable men and women in bottle-green uniforms. Some ministers form a close attachment to their drivers. Stan Orme's driver accompanied him almost everywhere, and was as familiar a figure at political drinkies as, say, Lady Falkender. Others don't get on so well. Dr David Owen had a bad reputation in all the car pools of Whitehall.

Anyway, early in his career, every minister has to make a choice: front or back? Front is friendlier, indicates that you are one of the lads, not ashamed to be seen hobnobbing with a mere chauffeur. Back provides the opportunity to think your own thoughts, read a paper-back thriller, even have a little drink.

My researches were carried out at the entrance to Downing Street, just as the weekly cabinet meeting ended. As each Rover sped past I noted the name and seat position of the occupant. One curious fact emerged. All the ministers who have detectives to protect them – such as Defence Secretary Francis Pym, Ulster Secretary, Humphrey Atkins and Home Secretary, Willie Whitelaw – were in the back. This is because the Special Branch likes its chaps to travel in front. Apart from them every single minister who went to public school – Michael Heseltine, Mark Carlisle, Lord Soames, Patrick Jenkin, David Howell – was in the front, often cheerily chatting away to the driver. The only one to sit in the back was the only one (apart from Heather herself) who went to grammar school – John Biffen, the Chief Secretary to the Treasury. What can this mean? Mr Biffen is probably the least pompous man I know. I suspect that he is actually too shy to talk to his driver.

The most touching sight was Lord Hailsham being whisked away in the front seat. His tiny dog, Mini, who has been his constant companion since his wife died last year, was leaping up and licking his face with delight. Lord Hailsham is one of the Cabinet's leading 'wets'. Mini, however, has been house-trained.

News of bon viveur Eddie Wainwright, the Labour MP for Dearne Valley, who makes every parliamentary delegation such an uproarious affair. He is just back from a visit to Three Mile Island, the site of the nuclear power station which nearly blew up last year. At the hotel in Washington he had been registered as Wayne E. Right, which is odd since Eddie is approximately one-third the size of the average Texan.

He has trouble sleeping in hotel rooms, and as usual spent most of the hours of darkness in the bar. On one occasion he was joined by a Tory MP on the delegation who had, at the time, a pocket full of toffee wrappers.

'Where's the bin?' the MP asked.

'Nowhere lad,' replied Wainwright, evidently in genuine puzzlement, 'ah've bin 'ere all the time.'

In June 1980, Dennis Skinner MP was sent out of the Commons chamber, for defying the Speaker.

The dismissal of Dennis Skinner, the Beast of Bolsover, the other day reminds me that the Beast is not always the one who dishes it out. Sometimes he gets it back. A few years ago, Jane Fonda was to address the Tribune group of left-wing Labour MPs on the subject of Vietnam. Skinner was sent to St Stephen's Entrance to meet her.

It was S⁺ Patrick's Day, and Skinner was wearing a spray of shamrock in his lapel. There was no sign of the fragile film star at St Stephen's Entrance, so someone suggested that she might, by mistake, have arrived in St Stephen's Tavern, the pub across the road from the Commons. Skinner nipped over, but couldn't see her there either. After shuttling to and fro between the two places he finally went up to the barmaid and asked, had she seen Jane Fonda? 'No, she usually sits over there with a bottle of Guinness, but she hasn't been in today. Now get out of here immediately, you drunken Irish git, before I call the police.'

By this time she had arrived, and the hapless Skinner even missed the beginning of her talk.

I have been hearing about Mr Benn's most extraordinary

obsession – himself. There is a TV room at the House of Commons where MPs can go to watch *Panorama*, *World In Action* or even *Dallas* if they so wish. It is equipped with a video-tape machine.

One evening a couple of Tory MPs went up to the room to watch the closing overs of the day's play in the Test Match. But they couldn't because the machine was in use, transmitting video-tapes of a Tony Benn speech to their admiring progenitor, who sat hunched in front of the screen carefully studying every phrase and gesture. The two MPs, slightly chagrined, left the room and mentioned what had happened, in some annoyance, to a third colleague.

The following morning the same chap tells me that a fourth Tory MP rushed up to him. 'Do you know,' he said, 'I just went upstairs to the TV room to watch the beginning

of the Test Match play, and I couldn't. That b— Tony Benn was sitting up their watching video-tapes of himself.'

The question now is, was Benn there all night? Quite possibly so.

Not all that long ago, he was appearing on an Open University TV programme about politics. Every time they tried to start recording, the sound man said that he was getting feedback and they couldn't go ahead until it was eliminated. After twenty minutes they found out what had happened. Tony Benn had switched the cassette-recorder, which he uses to tape every word he utters in public, on to 'playback' instead of 'record' and it was busily broadcasting his last speech to the waiting studio.

Absolutely guaranteed cast-iron true story about the heir to the throne, who seems to be even wittier than we had guessed. At a recent formal private dinner he confessed before his speech that he knew very little about the subject in question.

'In fact,' he said, 'I'm about as useful as Linda Lovelace with lockjaw.'

Hats off to Britain's social democratic pols, who have the guts to put their money where their convictions are! No fewer than three of the Gang of Four, David Owen, William Rodgers and Roy Jenkins have property within mushroom cloud distance of Greenham Common, one of the two sites for the American cruise missiles, and thus one of the two places targeted first for Soviet destruction.

Roy Jenkins lives at East Hendred, David Owen has a ramshackle old manor house at Buttermere, south of Newbury, and Rodgers has just bought a house at East Woodhay. Rodgers is perhaps the most courageous of the lot. First he takes on the Left by insisting that we do not disarm unilaterally, and then he goes to live in the path of an oncoming missile.

The devastation would be appalling, wiping out not only three-quarters of the SDP leadership, but also some of the finest wine in the country. One moment Roy Jenkins might be relaxing by the side of his tennis court, a chilled claret cup at his elbow, a copy of Roy Hattersley's amusing *Guardian* column in his hand. Then he looks up and sees the warhead from an SS-20 missile, shaped a little like a sawn-off ice-cream cone, dropping slowly, almost clumsily, towards him. Seconds later tennis court, Jenkins, claret and *Listener* are no more, reduced to their constituent protons, neutrons and electrons.

Another advantage of the SS-20 is that it has three warheads, each of which can be pinpointed on to a different target. If the missiles ever do come over, we will know the real reason – the Russians want to wipe out the SDP.

I heard some moving quotes recently from a Mr R. Bob Scoggin, the Grand Dragon of the Ku Klux Klan, and a man whose views on immigration and race relations clearly carry some weight. Mr Scoggin, who was attending a KKK rally in the United States, spoke to the reporter for the London *Daily Mail* and expressed the view that Margaret Thatcher was 'the only politician in the world'. She had, he said, 'changed the immigration laws to keep the darkies out' and would be more than welcome doing the same job in the United States.

The *Daily Mail* is usually only too keen to print the enthusiastic views of foreign statesmen such as Mr Scoggin. Yet for some reason, the quotes above failed to find their way into the *Mail* report, even though they were filed by its correspondent. I wonder why this should be? Certainly it was not for shortage of space, since the article showed every sign of having been 'leaded out' to fill an unexpected gap.

People still gleefully tell stories about Irene Ward. One of her most famous questions was about new uniforms for WRNS girls. The Navy Minister of the day replied that these would be dealt with as soon as the male officers and men had their new uniforms. Dame Irene was back in seconds: 'Is my right honourable friend saying,' she asked, 'that Wrens' skirts must be held up until all sailors have been satisfied?'

Nobody ever knew whether she was aware of what she was saying. I suspect she was. I recall her getting a big laugh by saying, 'Is the Minister aware that I have recently had a young soldier . . .'; long pause for effect before going on to say, 'write to me about. . .' She will be sorely missed.

Sir George Young, the tall, lager-drinking junior minister at the DHSS, recently attended an important ministers' meeting chaired by Lord Hailsham. Younger had been speaking for a time when Hailsham suddenly interrupted him.

'Shut up and come and sit on my knee!' the Lord Chancellor shouted.

It took the bemused Younger a minute or so to realize that Hailsham was addressing not him, but his adored pet dog, Mini.

I would have given a great deal to have attended the lunch at Chequers which the Prime Minister threw for her Scottish Tory MPs. There were a number of exquisite moments which will be savoured for months to come.

A few days before the lunch, which was on a Sunday, the MPs met at the Commons to decide how they should get to Chequers. A charabanc was suggested, though this was thought a trifle plebeian, even without a piano and a case of brown ale in the back. Quite a few of the Scottish Tories are ministers in one Department or another, and they suggested that if the occasion counted as official business, they could give lifts in their ministerial cars to their lower-ranking colleagues. At this point a message came from the House of Lords, where Lord Mansfield is a minister in the Scottish Office. It said that, with deep regret, he would be unable to offer a lift in his car, since Lady Mansfield would need to occupy the entire back seat so that her dress would not be crushed.

After the lunch, Heather set galumphing off to show the members and their wives her country pad (in fact one of her two country pads; she now has two official homes and two private ones). She led the way, the wives following in a bunch, and the chaps bringing up the rear.

One of the first sights they saw was the Walter Annenburg swimming pool, a gift to the nation, or at least to its leader, from the former American Ambassador. As his personal contribution to cutting public spending, Denis Thatcher has had the pool closed. It was costing £4,000 a year to heat, and only the staff were using it. Tough luck, staff.

I like the story told by Janet Morgan, the Oxford don who edited the Crossman diaries so magnificently, and is now a member of the Think Tank. Stepping out of Downing Street, she saw that a ministerial meeting was in progress in one Department or another, and the ministerial Rovers were lined up by the side of the road. Methodically working her way down the lot was a traffic warden, who was placing a ticket on each windscreen. Doctor Morgan explained politely to her that she was wasting her time, that was Sir Keith Joseph's car, that was the Chief Secretary to the Treasury's vehicle, and so forth. The warden's eyes blazed with the proud independence which made British traffic wardens the terrors of the world in the days of Empire.

'There's only one car in London I don't ticket,' she said, 'and that belongs to Her Majesty the Queen.'

Doubts about Mrs Thatcher's style persisted:

You can always tell that things are going horribly wrong when a Prime Minister has to start hiding things from her own Cabinet. The Cabinet, though it meets at least once a week and is nominally the principal decision-making body in the Government, is usually pretty badly informed about what is happening. As one minister said of the Callaghan Government: 'We're like mushrooms: we're kept in the dark all the time, and every now and again someone opens a door and throws a heap of manure all over us.' Still, they have the right to be told some things; not as much as the average viewer of, say, *Panorama* or *World In Action*, but enough to chew on when the Education Secretary has to make a decision about Afghanistan, or the Welsh Secretary has to provide his two penn'orth on North Sea oil.

I gather that Mrs Thatcher has now begun a series of top secret Inner Cabinet meetings, a charmed if not charming circle of blood-drinking monetarists such as Sir Keith Joseph, the Industry Secretary, Mr John Nott, the Trade Secretary, and Mr John Biffen, the Chief Secretary to the Treasury. These meetings are so secret that they are held at breakfast-time – when few of the public school chaps who belong to the Cabinet proper are awake – and are not even entered in her official diary of engagements, so that the secretaries and civil servants at Number 10 do not know about them. Most Prime Ministers retreat into a private *führerbunker* at some stage in their administration; it is unusual for them to do so quite so soon.

One thing she is absolutely marvellous about is looking after her backbenchers. Just as musicians and actors get to know the best landladies in every city, the ones who look after you and will give you bacon and eggs at one in the morning, so Tory MPs swear by her. If they could stand around in pubs with their colleagues saying, 'Great place to stop if you're ever near Downing Street, marvellous bloody woman, give you her address,' they would. They think (most of them) that she's terrific. Their wives tend to adore her.

Take the annual party for Tory MPs. Under Ted Heath this was thrown at some inconvenient time of year. Wives who wanted to come – that is, almost all of them – had to make a special trip down to London. Heath was often

100

late in arriving, sometimes by three-quarters of an hour. Frequently he looked bored and could hardly be bothered to chat to anyone. This was a fatal mistake. Most men will put up with any amount of rudeness to themselves, but will never forget or forgive a snub to their wives.

But Mrs Thatcher is perfect. For a start, she has changed the date of the party, indeed expanded it to three separate do's, held after each of the royal garden parties. This means that the wives, who have come down from their homes anyway, don't have to make a special trip. And she has perfected the art of making them feel at home. She remembers everybody's name and little personal details, e.g. 'Amanda, how marvellous to see you, what a lovely dress, I do hope your hamster is better.' It is a flinty-hearted woman who does not delight in such attention from the Prime Minister. Incidentally, it evokes a certain loyalty and respect from the husbands which her management of the country's affairs might fail to do.

More about Mrs Thatcher's social skills. One of her most persistent Tory rebels is Mr Geoffrey Dickens, the Fat Boy, who is, shall we say, less than totally committed in his support for each of the Government's policies. Indeed, for the Government, Mr Dickens is a pain in the neck. Recently he brought his mother down from Yorkshire to attend a party at Downing Street, and Mrs Thatcher spent no less than twenty minutes talking to them both, to the great jealousy of other MPs. What an incredibly sensible way of dealing with the people who have doubts about your policies.

She wasn't quite so successful at the reception for the England football team. At one point she was photographed holding a football aloft, and someone said in a stage whisper: 'At last she's got her hands where she wants them — on the strikers' balls.' Denis Thatcher, who must possess dozens if not hundreds of ties, contrived to appear wearing one in the design of a rugby club.

One of the pleasantest perks of being an MP is to go on

fact-finding visits. Naturally, fact-finding visits are very important. It is essential that our legislators are acquainted with the latest situation regarding tea prices in Ceylon, aircraft spares in Los Angeles, political unrest in the Caribbean, Common Market support for olive oil producers in Sicily, and the dangers in skiing holidays at St Moritz. Now and again they go somewhere unpleasant too, but this is usually tacked on to an urgent mission to some more agreeable and sunny clime.

It's easy enough to get on these things. The Commons is absolutely full of all-party committees covering just about every subject it is possible to imagine. Form an all-party Anglo-Seychelles committee, for instance, make yourself chairman, and within a few months the chances are you will be whisked off to that tropical paradise at the Seychelles' Government's expense. Join the all-party committee on cocoa processing, and weeks later you will be basking beneath the fronds on some West African beach.

What's more, there can be big prestige in it for you, as well as the free trips. Cocoa processing is bound to crop up in the news sooner or later, and you will have the thrill of sitting in the *World At One* studio listening to Robin Day saying: 'And one MP who feels strongly about the issue is Mr Christopher Swanning-Freeloader. . .' Or, 'One man just back from the turbulent islands in the Indian Ocean is. . .' Either way you win.

One marvellous example of this technique came up a few weeks ago, as four MPs, two Labour and two Tory, sat chatting in a bar discussing the forthcoming football match between England and Italy in Turin. They decided they would like to go. One of their number, Mr Keith Wickenden (Con, Dorking) is a director of Brighton and Hove Albion, and was deputed to find tickets. He was also elected chairman of the group. Mr Peter Snape (Lab, West Bromwich) was elected secretary, and Mr Richard Needham (Con, Chippenham) treasurer. Mr Jim Marshall (Lab. Leicester South) was elected to the committee.

The problem of getting there was solved just as easily.

The new committee decided to call itself the All-Party Committee on Football Hooliganism, so guaranteeing a free trip to Turin at the taxpayers' expense. They sat back and waited for the tickets.

Unfortunately, Mr Wickenden found he couldn't get them and, in the end, had another engagement. So the whole trip, which in reality was more a light-hearted joke than anything else, never took place. In the meantime, the four had told everyone about the All-Party Committee on Football Hooliganism, so it had become widely known and established.

Thus when there actually was a football riot in Italy, the four members of the group were deluged with phone calls from the BBC and commercial stations demanding their comments on the appalling scenes. In such a way does fact catch up, panting slightly, with fiction.

It was a close-run thing, but Parliament finished just before the Glorious Twelfth, and our more sporting legislators were able to speed north for the annual slaughter of edible winged creatures. It has always struck me as an exceedingly expensive way of getting food. If they want the pleasure of shooting, why don't they use clay pigeons, which can be fired off almost anywhere and are a lot cheaper? And if it is nutrition they seek, why don't they raise battery grouse and have the fun and pleasure of going round breaking their necks? I don't see much of a difference, and it could be made to last all year.

Be that as it may, shooting has always had a central part in our political life. Up to the last century, Parliament never even sat when the shooting season was open. The great jibe against Harold Macmillan and Alec Douglas-Home was that they were 'grouse moor politicians'. Willie Whitelaw himself likes to go shooting. They proudly tell the story at Scotland Yard about one of his Special Branch detectives who was assigned to guard him while on a shoot somewhere on the Scottish moors. Out of curiosity, Willie asked the detective if he thought he could shoot a bird with his pistol – a fairly remarkable feat. The Inspector said he'd have a go, raised his small firearm and hit the beast, shattering it into tiny fragments of flesh.

Willie, astonished by this display of marksmanship, excitedly called over his host to view the remains. The Laird looked disapprovingly at the plumage, blood and bone, then drily remarked, 'Hmm, I suppose it will do for soup.'

MPs are by and large, a fairly clean bunch. I don't quite know why, but it may be because they are always in danger of meeting a constituent. If someone has journeyed from Scotland to meet his member, he may well be distinctly put off by seeing and sniffing someone caked in dried sweat. Equally, Mr Speaker might well be disinclined to call someone who has a cluster of small flies buzzing round his head. Working in that stuffy building in summer is demanding in many ways, and a proper attention to personal hygiene is essential.

Jim Callaghan, for example, likes to sauna. During the notorious Labour Party meeting at which the ludicrous commission of inquiry came to its various preposterous conclusions, the Opposition Leader spent every break he could in the sauna. Unfortunately, there were no naked Finnish women with birch twigs to attend him; instead he had the company of Mr Ian Mikardo, who is about as different in appearance from a naked Finnish woman as it is possible for any living creature to be while remaining a member of the same species.

Mr Dennis Skinner, the Beast of Bolsover, paid a rare – possibly his only – visit abroad before he became an MP. He went on a tour of the Soviet Union. At one point the party visited a mine and, on regaining the pithead, were taken to the bathouse. Here Skinner saw that the person who was to wash his naked form was an immense Russian woman wielding a brush almost as tall as herself. Skinner, unwashed, fled.

So that MPs may keep themselves as delightfully clean and fresh as the people who appear in, say, adverts for toilet paper, the authorities have installed a shower in the House. A while ago two MPs, one Tory and one Labour, were showering there at the same time.

Mr Tristan Garel-Jones (Con, Watford) addressed miner Mr Mick Welsh (Lab, Don Valley) thus: 'Do you know, Mick, us public school chaps and you miners have got one thing in common.'

Mr Welsh responded interrogatively: 'Aye?'

'Well, both public school boys and miners take their showers together, with other people.'

There was a long pause while the water hissed down and gurgled into the plug hole. 'Aye,' said Mr Welsh again, 'but *we* can risk bending down to pick up the soap.'

During the so-called Winter of Discontent, while all of Britain was suffering from the absence of trains, lorries and rubbish collections, and with the temperature at or below freezing, I was lucky enough to be in Los Angeles.

As I sped towards my assignment in a rented Ford Fairmount (automatic transmission, power-steering, electronic ash tray), there were palm trees on my left and the glittering Pacific ocean on my right. The temperature was around 55 degrees Fahrenheit. I selected the FM stereo band on the car radio and punched the button for the CBS all-news station.

A voice said, urgently, as if announcing the outbreak of World War III, 'In Britain, Premier James Callaghan has come under heavy criticism in the Parliament for attending the Guadeloupe summit of world leaders while Britain faces its most devastating ever series of strikes by labor unions. One member of the Parliament called it "the worst political decision since Caligula made his horse a consul". Another accused Premier Callaghan of being like Emperor Nero and fiddling while Rome was burning.'

All this must have been very dull stuff to the few thousand Angelenos who heard it, but it almost made me crash the car into a palm tree. For there, through the miracles of modern technology, six thousand miles away, I was hearing one of the great performances of the House of Commons Repertory Company.

For a theatrical group which plays to so many people, it is surprising how few have actually heard of the Commons Rep. Yet it is ever present. It has, perhaps, a dozen or twenty members. You could be listening to the *Jimmy Young Show*, and at 11 o'clock the news headlines begin: 'Labour MPs have lashed out at a Conservative council's decision to remove soft toilet paper from school lavatories. MP Mr Gwilym Roberts said. . .'

Or even the *Nine O'Clock News* might have an item: 'Tory MPs have been angered by what they see as unjustified support for striking paper doily manufacturers from the Labour Opposition. The MP for Edgbaston, Mrs Jill Knight, said that the striking doily workers were "holding the country to ransom. . ." '

Provincial papers tend to carry slabs from the Rep when their regular Lobby Correspondent is too busy or is away on holiday. 'Labour MPs yesterday said, "Hands off the marmoset." Wolverhampton MP Mrs Renee Short wants a full House of Commons inquiry into the threat to marmoset breeding in the West Midlands. She said yesterday. . .' The Rep sometimes keeps entire local radio stations going. 'A shock call for Prince Charles to become a Jehovah's Witness came yesterday from Louth Tory MP Mr Michael Brotherton. Mr Brotherton said that the sooner the heir to the throne started going from door to door, meeting people and refusing blood transfusions the better. A political correspondent says that Mr Brotherton's shock call will shock many Tory leaders. . .'

Notice the way that the Rep's contributions are always presented as shock horrors. In fact, for Mr Brotherton (a personally charming man, as many will testify) to say something mildly bonkers is no more unusual than for Sir Geoffrey Howe to say something mildly boring. If it were Mrs Thatcher, or even a more obscure MP who gets taken seriously such as Mr Peter Tapsell or Sir William van Straubenzee, then it would indeed be worthy of note. Since it is Mr Brotherton it is about as newsworthy as Richard Burton getting drunk — mildly interesting at best, utterly predictable at worst.

The Rep has no formal rules. Many of its members do not really know each other. They tend to operate through the Press Association, whose hard-working correspondents jot down their thoughts, and phone them to the PA offices, whence they arrive on the newsdesks of a thousand local papers and radio stations. Sometimes the PA correspondent will obligingly invent the quotes for the MP, phoning him back to make sure they are acceptable. On other occasions, the PA man will actually prepare parliamentary questions or motions, which the MP can take to the Table Office for printing, secure in the knowledge that what he has signed is far more likely to get extensive press coverage than anything he might have written himself.

The Rep seems, for some reason, to have more members on the Tory side than with Labour. This is partly because

Labour MPs tend to specialize, to stick to the Royal Family or the Evils of Multi-National Corporations, whereas your true Rep member, like an eldery character actor, can turn his mouth to anything, from underweight ice-cream cones to the threat to world peace. For this reason, Rep members tend to be looked down on by their colleagues, who point out correctly that few of the Rep ever get Government jobs. Nobody takes them seriously. Yet Rep MPs remain unconcerned. One Tory member, who has a fairly but not very safe seat, told me it did wonders for him in his constituency. 'They hear my views every day on the radio, and they think the sun shines out of my backside,' he said.

Sometimes the Rep does have a useful function. Years ago, in late 1974, at least half the Tory Party thought it was time for Ted Heath to go, but the Conservative code of 'omerta', or silence, forbade any of them to say so.

Then, to the rescue, came Mr Nicholas Winterton, the Tory MP for Macclesfield, and one of the Rep's most distinguished members. He bounced into the House to start work early one morning, announced to the Press Association chap that it was time Ted Heath cleared off, and the first crack in the dam had appeared. Normally Mr Winterton's views do not count for very much. On this occasion, since he had merely said what everybody else thought, they counted for a great deal.

One of the saddest sights it is possible to see is a Rep member who has lost his seat. What must it be like, for instance, to be Mr William Molloy, the Labour MP for Ealing who was ousted from the Company in the 1979 election? To have all these opinions about site value rating, nuclear submarines, quality control for doughnuts and the menace of pornographic videotapes and nowhere to put them? Colonel Marcus Lipton, who died while MP for Brixton, was the doyen of the Rep for many years, and it is suspected that he is still in touch with the Press Association through an ouija board.

Perhaps past members still sidle up to people in pubs

and say, 'You know old chap, in a shock statement I am lashing out at beer prices. It is an outrage that the working man should pay more for his pint than the average miner earns in 45 minutes. I shall be tabling a shock letter in my local newspaper. . .' But nobody is listening, for the other customers have quietly turned away to play the Pac-Man machine, leaving the former MP with only a lingering sense of his former faded glory.

Now and again, and rather more often these days, Conservative MPs like to play the bus game. The game consists in asking, 'If Mrs Thatcher were run over by a Number 11 bus tomorrow, who would you pick as leader?' Not long ago the Young Conservatives, at one of their conferences, held a poll on this question. Several possible successors were mentioned. I think Jim Prior got around 20 per cent, Lord Carrington 18 per cent, Geoffrey Howe 5 per cent, and so on. The winner however, with 49 per cent, was 'the driver of the bus'.

Sir Keith Joseph, I learn, has now found nemesis in the shape of a youthful punk (or it may be a mod, or a rude boy). The punk lives in the same street as Sir Keith. The former Industry Secretary is separated from his wife, though still lives near her, and has to do his own shopping. Every now and then he takes his bag down to the local supermarket to lay in supplies of eggs, smoked salmon and the few other items which appear on his limited diet. Frequently when he does the punk assails him, like some avenging angel from the working classes, saying in broad Cockney, decorated with many colourful expletives, "Worrabaht the unemployed, Sir Keef, worrabaht 'em, uh?' and similar political messages.

Say what you will about Sir Keith, he is a man of boundless courtesy and an intense desire to pass on the truths he has learned to others. So instead of telling the punk to get lost, or calling the police, he enters into an intellectual economic and philosophical argument with

Sir Keith Joseph

him, earnestly pointing out the punk's mistakes. Frequently these exchanges end with friendly mutual abuse.

On one occasion the punk's mother was appalled, when giving her son a lift in the car, to see him make rude gestures at Sir Keith from the passenger seat. She was even more astonished when Sir Keith made equally agitated gestures back. On another occasion the punk challenged Sir Keith on the appointment of Ian MacGregor as Chairman of the British Steel Corporation.

The burden of his plaint was that MacGregor was paid too much, that it had cost too much to buy him back from America, and that Sir Keith had made a terrible decision. Sir Keith pointed out that there was a committee which would oversee the BSC and report if MacGregor was making a terrible botch of his job. The punk pointed out that the committee was drawn from the usual ranks of Government and industry and was, in fact, a fix. Sir Keith could then be seen by all the neighbours bellowing down the street, 'Take that back! You must take that back!' as the punk sauntered merrily away.

What Sir Keith may not realize is that this terrifying figure, this witch's familiar set to haunt his waking moments, is no ordinary yob. He is instead one Sammy Miller, the highly intelligent and well-educated son of famous literary critic and editor Karl Miller. The workers will finally cast off their chains in many strange ways and through many unexpected means.

One Fleet Street editor of my acquaintance is notoriously mean with his cigarettes and notoriously quick to bum them from other people. There is, I am told, a sign in the Gents at his newspaper which reads: 'Please do not throw your cigarette butts into the urinal. The editor finds them difficult to light.'

To the Bedford Hotel, Brighton to attend the most boring political meeting ever held. It was organized by the Tory Unity Group as a fringe event at the Party Conference.

The Unity Group is supposed to be full of right-wing beasties who want to introduce capital punishment in primary schools and use selective torture as a means of ending strikes. To judge by the gathering I saw, this lot couldn't organize a counter-revolution in a Brownie pack. It was as silent and somnolent as a grave-digger's siesta.

It wasn't helped by the Chairman, Mr George Gardiner, the cadaverous MP for Reigate. Though he is just about the head beastie on the Tory Right, he has a boring voice, like a chain-saw winding down. This has a narcotic, comatose effect on his listeners. At the beginning of his speech he grated, 'I do not wish to use this occasion to make a personal attack on Jim Prior.'

'Why not?' asked somebody, reasonably enough. After that it was downhill all the way. Two men in front of me fell fast asleep and began snoring loudly. I saw Sir Robin Day's head start to nod gently and his eyes to close. As speaker after speaker droned on, the whole room seemed to sway in gentle sympathy, as if afflicted with Legionnaire's Disease. One man called on Mr Prior 'to expose himself'. But even this fluff, usually a trigger for any British audience to fall around in helpless laughter, went unnoticed and unremarked. I tottered out over the slumbering bodies in search of something more enlivening to do, such as staring at my fingernails for half-an-hour on the pier.

One star speaker at the conference proper was a young Oxford student called William Hague (no relation to the acid-bath murderer of the same name). A few years ago young William electrified the conference, shortly before he reached puberty, through a speech resonant with clichés and elderly saws. Afterwards, as the delegates rose to give him a standing ovation and Mrs Thatcher leaned forward to congratulate him, Lord Carrington whispered to his neighbour, Norman St John-Stevas, 'if he's like that now, what on earth will he be like in 20 years time?'

Norman answered, 'Michael Heseltine?'

The Tory Party usually manages to organize its debates with superb efficiency. Dissent is stifled, amendments ig-

112

nored, everything arranged to provide a seamless impression of calm moderation. The party managers miss no tiny detail, including the fact that the daily conference TV coverage is interrupted at 11 every morning for a children's programme. This means that hundreds of thousands of housewives are watching the box in the few minutes before the kiddy slot begins. Naturally it is vital that these people, many of them floating voters, see a dignified speech by a senior Tory leader, not some crazed loony from the constituencies who wants to bring back hanging, drawing and quartering.

To this end there is a woman whose job it is to pass a note to the Chairman at around 10.45, warning him that the key moment is imminent. A year or so back it was Keith Joseph who was on his feet, and the Chairman noticed that he was nearing the end of an extremely short speech. He passed him a note: 'You must keep going until 11 o'clock.' Joseph, never the sanest looking or sounding individual, suddenly slowed down to a crawl, slurring each word, leaving long pauses between syllables, altogether giving the appearance of a man totally demented. Thousands of housewives must have fled the party in terror.

Mrs Thatcher, I gather, spent the entire conference on a total high, the effect of power on her being similar to that of cocaine on a film starlet. People brought back reports of her manic energy, the demoniacal gleam in her wild yet purposeful eyes. At the *Blue Revue*, a less than sparkling satire on modern politics (every year the Tory Party has a revue attacking Labour politicians; in reply most years the Labour conference also mounts a revue attacking Labour politicians) she insisted on leaping on to the stage in mid-performance.

At the Young Conservatives' Ball (always the social highlight of the season, distinguished this year by Mr Norman St John-Stevas actually appearing on the platform with a mysterious young woman in black sequins) she arrived early, and before anyone could stop her had launched into her own energetic version of Apache dancing, swirling round the floor like a Toulouse-Lautrec painting before drawing the raffle prize. All of this was a little hurtful to the Lord Privy Seal (or Seal as he is universally known) Sir Ian Gilmour, who had understood that he was to lead off the dancing with the Prime Minister. But though he and Lady Gilmour arrived on time, she had already danced off into the night, leaving the Gilmours to take a quiet and reflective drink on their own in an upstairs bar.

My favourite delegate at the Tory conference was the one who spoke in the debate on water authorities, which followed the debates on industry and agriculture.

'I may not know about industry or about agriculture, but when it comes to water I can certainly hold my own.'

With surprising exaggeration, in the same debate, a delegate solemnly said, 'When the name of the East Anglian Water Authority is heard, it is the terror of the country.'

I wonder whom Mr Harold Macmillan is backing for the leadership of the Labour Party this year? Last time, I gather, he was a keen enthusiast for Mr Tony Benn. He told friends chatting to him at the Carlton Club – where he provides welcome relief from the tedious businessmen who go there nowadays – that Benn was the most likely to smash the Labour Party. When Benn dropped out, he said, he switched allegiance to Michael Foot on the grounds that he was the second most likely to smash the Labour Party. The hooded eyes drooped lower, the hands plucked fretfully at the walking stick, then some young man asked earnestly: 'But sir, what about the country?'

Macmillan replied, 'Don't you worry about the country, dear boy, the country is beyond recall. You stick to the party.'

James Callaghan resigned the leadership of the Labour Party in October 1980. Immediately, various TV programmes began to run polls to discover how MPs would vote for his successor.

The trophy for the Most Fat-Headed Polling must go, *summa cum laude*, to the *Nationwide* programme. They telephoned a young MP called Michael Ancram to ask which Labour leader he would be voting for. Not only is Ancram the next Marquis of Lothian, he is the Tory MP for Edinburgh South and the present chairman of the Scottish Conservative Party.

When leadership elections crop up, MPs lovingly repeat to each other one of their favourite stories, turning it round and admiring its glitter, like a miser fondling a two-ounce Krugerrand. When Harold Wilson retired, Roy Hattersley thought long and hard and decided that, much as he admired his two friends and colleagues Roy Jenkins and Tony Crosland, he would have to give his support to Jim Callaghan.

115

So he called round to see Jenkins at the Home Office. He explained his deep and lasting respect for him, his personal friendship, but his feeling that the party required unity above all and that this could be furnished only by Callaghan. Jenkins listened sympathetically, said how well he appreciated Hattersley's dilemma and how much he admired his honesty for coming to tell him. The two men then enjoyed a glass of wine with a conversation about old times and the future.

Pleased with this civilized meeting, Hattersley made his next visit to the Department of the Environment where Crosland was Secretary of State. As they sat at the top of those hideous towers from which the despoliation of Britain is presently organized, Hattersley again sketched out his reasoning, the difficulty of his choice, his friendship – almost reverence – for Crosland. After he had finished, Crosland drew on his cigar and said, 'Thank you, Roy, for your honesty and candour in coming to see me and telling me this. I appreciate it very greatly. Now piss off.'

The only thing wrong with this absolutely true story is that when Hattersley got to the bottom of the lift the receptionist at the door had a message for him. It was an apology from Crosland.

I write before knowing the result of the final ballot for next leader of the Labour Party. I can report, however, that the left-wing candidate Michael Foot, once described by the late Jeremy Thorpe as the only man in the House of Commons to make his own shoes, has again attracted the admiration and support of Mr Enoch Powell. Shortly after Foot's superbly funny speech on unemployment, Powell leaned over to his neighbour, a Labour MP, and said, 'A brilliant speech. It was a devastating attack on the Government which never once strayed into the shoals of offering an alternative policy.'

I can also exclusively reveal Mrs Thatcher's preference in this election. Shortly after the first ballot was announced last week, the Prime Minister ran by chance into an unusually jaunty Denis Healey in a Commons corridor. She congratulated him warmly on coming top of the poll and added with a charming smile, 'Oh I do hope you get it in the end!'

Denis, a mite grudgingly, replied, 'Oh, do shut up. I got Peter Thorneycroft's endorsement on TV the other day and that was quite enough.'

MPs began to collect Keith Joseph stories:

Poor Keith Joseph is rapidly becoming the despair of his keepers. We all know the man is within reach of his ambition – to complete the total destruction of British industry – but he might at least keep up the pretence of wanting the opposite. Granada TV technicians are still relishing an interview he gave on the day the new Mini-Metro was launched.

It began with the interviewer asking him if he didn't think the Metro was a marvellous new wonder-car and the salvation of the British motor industry. Sir Keith replied simply, 'I don't know.' Well, the interviewer tried, didn't it lead the field, outstrip the foreign competition, set new standards and so on? Sir Keith said gloomily, 'You're asking the wrong man.' In the silence that followed, the interviewer tried a third time. As Secretary for Industry, didn't Sir Keith welcome... His subject said unhappily, 'You see, I'm not a car man. I haven't even owned a car since mine was stolen five years ago.'

By now near total despair, the interviewer made one final effort. Surely, he asked, Sir Keith had ridden in the car, had had a chance to try out the controls? There was another long and agonized pause. 'Well, I haven't really, I haven't seen, I don't know ... oh dear, you'll have to stop, I've lost my grammar.' This ringing morale-boosting endorsement of British engineering achievement was, curiously enough, never broadcast.

Mr Joel Barnett, Chief Secretary to the Treasury in the last Labour Government, and lately campaign manager for the Chancellor of the Exchequer in that same Government, burst into the room where the leadership results were about to be announced last week, and breathlessly approached Mr Ian Mikardo, the House of Commons' resident bookie.

'Thank goodness I've found you. I want to put a fiver on Denis now,' he panted.

'But the result's being declared in 30 seconds,' Mikardo replied, wondering if Mr Barnett had surreptitiously gained inside knowledge.

It doesn't matter. Just put it on,' the tiny accountant said. Moments later Mr Mikardo pocketed the easiest £5 he had ever earned while reflecting on just why the Treasury was run with such conspicuous lack of success between 1974 and 1979.

One problem for Michael Foot is that while he is a marvellously vigorous journalist and a platform orator of a style and fervour few people can match these days he isn't so well adapted to the modern media. For example he can't read out anything that's written down without sounding forced and wooden.

Take the famous line when he said that his wife had threatened him with divorce if he did not stand for the leadership. It was meant to be a joke, but he read it in such a flat monotonous voice that some of his listeners thought he meant it. Reporters were despatched round to meet this fearsome virago whose lightest word was law. Instead they found a charming, amusing, ever-so-slightly scatty woman who would no more issue diktats or fiats to her husband than she would vote Conservative. Jill Foot was asked about her role in the affair. 'Oh dear, all these terrible journalists saying that I forced him into standing. I can't even force him into buying a new suit.'

No wonder that he looks faintly dotty on television. As Mr Kenneth Baker, smooth-tongued Tory MP for Marylebone, the only man in the Commons with spray-on hair,

Michael Foot

said the day after the election: 'The Labour Party has just been led by Dixon of Dock Green. Now it's being led by Worzel Gummidge.' Baker was, I believe, the first man to coin this sobriquet.

Foot's crumpled suit and battered shoes seem unlikely to change. After all, you can't take a morning constitutional on Hampstead Heath each day in some Italian mohair and polyester number with two-tone soft leather shoes. Incidentally, the plastic shield he wears attached to the left side of his glasses is to protect the eye. When he was Leader of the House he suffered from a painful attack of shingles, which left the eye permanently impaired, and susceptible to draughts.

He has great difficulty in performing for the telly. Interviewers and producers wanting to demonstrate his charm will ask him to chat easily to party workers, constituents, or even his next-door neighbour in Ebbw Vale, Mrs Lily Tagg. 'Now Mike, sweety, can we just have two minutes of you chatting at your ease to Mrs Tagg?' the producer will say. Foot, ever willing to oblige, will stump out of his tiny terrace house and bang on next door's knocker. Mrs Tagg answers. 'Hello, all right?' he barks, 'Yes, thank you,' says Mrs Tagg. 'Very good,' says Foot, turning to the cameras and saying, 'Is that enough for you?' The man is almost incapable of dissembling. It would be untrue to say that he is as honest as the day is long, but he seems to manage it for more than 23 hours.

Incidentally, it turns out that 'Foot' is the popular slang word in Romanian for sexual intercourse. I learn from the BBC in Bush House that broadcasters in their Romanian service have been queueing up to read the bulletins about the Labour leadership.

Keen young Gary Gibbon of Harrow (the suburb, not the school) has an unusual hobby, a pastime which some might think positively perverted. He collects signed photographs of Cabinet Ministers. I know a few people who would sooner collect wombat droppings, yet as a hobby Gary's has much to recommend it. It is extremely cheap, it is very easy and it makes a lot of eldery people very happy.

This *aficionado* has been kind enough to lend me a few recent gems from his collection. At first, as one riffles through the pictures *en masse*, the impression is at once dizzying and nauseous. As one looks more closely, however, the effect is touching and slightly pathetic; as those brave, determined smiles gleam off the glossy paper one realizes how pleased and flattered the victims must have been to get such a request.

All the pictures are signed, and some are accompanied by chatty little notes. Mr Patrick Jenkin's secretary says that he was 'only too pleased to autograph the enclosed photograph'. Sir Ian Gilmour has 'the greatest pleasure' in sending his picture. Mr St John-Stevas's press officer is fulsome.

In fact the snap of Norman is the best in the bunch. He has that 'aren't I a lad?' look on his face, so the picture resembles one of those endless adverts in the Stage newspaper for failing comics one has never quite heard of. His name should appear with a catch phrase in the middle thus: Best Seasonal Wishes to All My Fans – Norman 'Your Round I Think!' St John-Stevas – Star of TV's 'Cor Strike A Light' – now in Puss-in-Boots, Masonic Rooms, Godalming.

The picture of the Home Secretary shows Willie gazing oyster-eyed into the middle distance. It is clearly designed to imply a visionary Whitelaw few of us know, but the general effect is to resemble the chaps in those Fifties movies who scoffed at the idea of flying saucers then saw one land next door.

Mark Carlisle's photo has been lovingly pasted on to brown cardboard so that it may be stood up on a dresser, like a wedding picture. Francis Pym's likeness is minute, as if clipped out of a Polyfoto sheet, whereas John Biffen's is huge, as large as a film poster.

The signatures are revealing as well. Lord Hailsham has written, underneath a picture of himself in full wig and robes, in an almost Gothic script, of the kind one imagines Henry VIII used for signing Anne Boleyn's death warrant. Michael Heseltine has scrawled over his pic the letters 'Michael R'. Not yet, Mike old chap, not yet.

What a conceited bunch they all are. I'm sure if there is any more vainglorious body of men in the world than Conservative ministers, it is Labour ministers.

In Autumn we had a US president, a new Labour Party leader, and learned that Kirstin had shot J. R. Ewing. Remember Dallas?

I gather that Mr Denis Healey is not taking his defeat in the Labour leadership election at all well. Indeed he is going about looking as grumpy and ill tempered as a man who had a £10 accumulator bet on Michael Foot, Ronald Reagan and Sue-Ellen. And furthermore he is being perfectly beastly to the new leader.

For example, he is endeavouring to run Shadow Cabinet meetings as if it were he who had won the election. He keeps chipping in and attempting to change the subject under discussion. After each little debate he will aggressively sum up the mood of the meeting. He seems to have a compulsive need to say whatever is on his mind the moment that it crosses that awesome threshold. He throws his weight about continually.

Now one of Mr Healey's most attractive characteristics is that, while a bully, he doesn't mind who he bullies. He is perfectly prepared to take on someone his own size, or even larger. The Leader of the Labour Party is a fairly hefty target, and while it was another substantial bruiser like Jim Callaghan, nobody minded. In fact they rather enjoyed it.

But frail, lovable, snowy-haired old Michael Foot does not come into the same Dreadnought class. Bullying him is like shouting abuse at the elderly gents who sit feeding squirrels in the park, or stealing their free bus passes. People don't like it. They think it puts Mr Healey in a bad light.

No one can work out why the Blob is so rough. People assume it isn't simply the canker of jealousy marring the rose of his otherwise flawless character. Can it be, they ask themselves, that Denis hopes that Michael will finally crack, throw in his stick and return to his collected Hazlitt? Or has he decided that all is not actually lost? If Labour were to fail at the next election, Healey would still be younger than Foot is now. Might not a desperate party admit its mistake and turn, once again, to the Blob? Personally I doubt it. I think they'd vote for Mr Peter Shore who, whatever his shortcomings, is well mannered in a way that would delight Miss Emily Post.

An even greater dislike is that felt by Michael Foot for his putative challenger, Tony Benn. After Benn had made a highly tendentious speech at the Labour conference, in which he wrongly accused Jim Callaghan of dumping manifesto commitments, Foot was seen distinctly mouthing to him, as he sat down, the words 'fucking liar'. Someone later challenged him about this. Foot vehemently denied using the words. 'What I said to him was "fucking lies",' he riposted.

I ran into a worried looking Labour MP the other day. 'If

Peter Shore

jensen

the party leader gave a plaster cast of his foot to charity,' he asked me, 'what would the Chief Whip, Michael Cocks, give?'

A couple of splendid Willie Whitelawisms have just reached me. The Home Secretary was speaking in the debate on the European Assembly Elections Bill, a tedious piece of legislation concerned with electoral boundary changes. Mr Whitelaw was defending some obscure and arcane decision by the Government.

A Labour MP rose indignantly from the bench. 'You voted against that last time!' he shouted. Willie did not bat a bushy eyebrow or wobble a single jowl.

'That,' he declared, 'does not alter the logic of my position.'

He was in more waspish mood when they brought news to him that Mr Foot had appointed Roy Hattersley as Shadow Home Secretary. There are two versions of his reaction; one, put about by friends of Mr Hattersley, is that Willie disappeared down a corridor gibbering with terror. This version is not true. What actually happened is that he groaned and said, 'I could take a man who was straight left. I could stand someone who was straight right. But Hattersley is neither left, right, nor straight.'

A deeply sad and probably true story: Geoffrey Dickens, Tory MP for Huddersfield, used to be the most unpopular new Member. With his blunt 'where there's muck there's brass' approach, his habit of throwing his considerable weight about and his practice of voting with the Opposition, he made more enemies in a couple of months than most people manage in a political lifetime. Now, however, he has been rehabilitated, and his genial manner has made him one of the most sought-after companions in the Smoking Room, where recently he told this tragic tale about himself.

A while ago he was opening a fête in his constituency. As he moved from coconut shy to tombola to sale of work he was followed everywhere by a spectacularly ugly woman. Every time he looked up he would see her smiling at him and, embarrassed, would smile back, rapidly returning to the business in hand.

A few days later he received a letter, evidently from the woman. It said how much she admired him and asked whether perhaps he had noticed her at the fête. Would he be so kind as to send her an autographed photo of himself? The letter was signed with the woman's name, after which came in brackets the word 'Horseface.'

Clearly this was a nickname she had either invented for herself or had wished upon her, and her brave use of it indicated that this was how she came to terms with her physical disfigurement. Dickens was filled with admiration for such courage and decided to go to town on the photograph. He bought a special frame, signed the king-size picture of himself 'Best Wishes Horseface, from Geoffrey Dickens', parcelled it up and sent it off.

The next day he ran into his secretary. She asked, 'did you get that letter from the really ugly woman? I wrote "Horseface" after her name on the letter so you'd know which one she was.'

Mrs Thatcher sacked some and moved others of her ministers in January 1981.

The mysteries of Mrs Thatcher's cack-handed reshuffle (one parliamentary wag, in his letter of condolence to the saintly St John-Stevas, said that his nickname for her, the 'Leaderene', should now be changed to the 'wolverine') continue to deepen. Like ancient alchemists, MPs find themselves endlessly searching for the key that will dispel their ignorance and reveal the secret of her intentions. Is it to do with sex? they ask. Is membership of obscure and possibly disloyal dining clubs the link between the victims? Have all of them given offence to Ian Gow, her parliamentary private secretary, known universally as 'Super-grass'? Certainly it seems to have nothing to do with competence or the lack of it.

One wretched chap, who took his phone call from Heather after he had just arrived at a ski resort, determined not to let it spoil his holiday. When he returned a week later he found a letter from the Lady. It was positively eulogistic in tone. He had been a marvellous minister, in one of the most effective teams she had, and had been 'a real asset to the Government'. What can she mean? The poor fellow is seeking a meeting with her, but I doubt if it will bring him much enlightenment.

Of course, prime ministers find this business so embarrassing that they like to pretend that they are not their own masters but driven by external forces outside their control. They can never bring themselves to say, 'I am sacking you because you're useless' or 'because you've been carrying on with your secretary' or 'because I owe a few favours to the NUM'.

One bright Labour backbencher was terribly hurt in March 1974 when Harold Wilson did not give him the job he had expected. So he did the approved thing, which is to seek a meeting with the Chief Whip. As he walked in, Bob Mellish, who held that post at the time, said, 'Harold wants you to know that he thinks you've been very hard done by.' The MP reeled out of the room in astonishment. He was luckier than most, and actually got a job in October that year.

A spy tells me about a rare meeting, at some recent state function, of three former Prime Ministers, Messrs Heath, Callaghan and Macmillan. At one point Macmillan pointed out that there are now so many ex-prime ministers alive (the actual total is five, including Lord Home and Sir Harold Wilson) that they could form a Government of their own.

'And,' he added slyly and slowly, to general approval, 'we wouldn't have any women in it, would we?'

I am quite certain that Mrs Thatcher would not have promoted one of her ministers if she had known that he has been trying to coin a new meaning for her name. He has been in the habit of going into bars at, say, seven o'clock and saying, 'Give me a large brandy and soda, will you, I've had a thatcher of a day!' Or when people invite him to a convivial social gathering, he will say, 'No, I'm terribly sorry, but I feel absolutely thatchered.' I will undertake not to name this disloyal young fellow, provided that he sends me a large cheque made out to the Save St John-Stevas For The Nation Fund.

Incidentally, some of the tributes which attended Mr Stevas's sacking (like Mark Twain, and more recently Ngaio Marsh, he has had the exquisite pleasure of seeing his own obituaries in print) made the mistake of assuming that he had invented all the nicknames in current use at Westminster. Just as witty phrases in turn-of-the-century London society tended to get attributed to Oscar Wilde, and later any political joke be ascribed to Winston Churchill, so any decent nickname was credited to Norm. He did invent the 'Leaderene' and the 'Blessed One' (the 'Sainted One' refers to Princess Margaret). He did coin 'Niglet' for Nigel Lawson, the thick-set cream-suited Energy Minister who dresses, according to one of his colleagues, 'like an Armenian might for a holiday in Florida'. He was the first to point out how much Lord Carrington looks like Kermit the Frog.

But several other popular sobriquets, such as 'Geoffrey Who?' for the Chancellor, 'Ong-goose', the French pronunciation of Angus Maude's first name, and 'John Nitt' for the Defence Secretary, are all the work of another well-known wet, Sir Ian Gilmour. Sir Ian, one of our most debonair and gifted cabinet ministers, deserves the credit for these, and I am delighted to be able to offer it.

There has been much snorting at Westminster over Lord George-Brown's recent unpleasant appearance on the Parkinson show. Among his many extraordinary remarks the

128

bibulous former Foreign Secretary said that Harold Wilson was the only man in the Commons who could not walk from A to B in a straight line. This is a curious allegation from the man who, on the day he resigned from the Labour Party, found it impossible to walk across the road without falling into the gutter.

At one point he sneered that the Labour Party should not be led by someone who had one eye and one leg. An angry friend of Michael Foot's commented, 'Ah well, in the country of the legless the one-legged man is king.'

The other day Michael Mates, the agreeable Tory MP for Petersfield and aide-de-camp to Willie Whitelaw, was ruefully recounting an incident which took place in Covent Garden. He had lunched at the Garrick Club and as he was leaving he spotted Sir Robin Day waiting for a cab. Naturally he offered him a lift to the House, but when they got to the bay, they found its exit blocked by a huge furniture van which was unloading vast quantities of the chi-chi tat which is sold in that part of London, macramé cocktail cabinets, neo-Georgian light-dimmers and so forth. (I once saw a set of video-cassette holders, bound in leather with eighteenth-century style gold tooling, tricked out to look like a shelf of books.)

'Excuse me,' said a friend of Mates to the lorry driver, 'but we have to get this car out to go to the House of Commons. Would you mind moving for a moment?' The driver made it clear, in the colourful language of the London streets, that he would mind very much. Mates tried himself. 'Look, I have to take Sir Robin Day to the House of Commons. Please would you move your van?'

'Robin Day?' said the man, 'why didn't you say so?' With which he hopped into his cab and zoomed away.

'Twenty-five years ago,' said Mates, 'I'd have given him my name and what's more, he'd have known who I was.'

In 1981 the Labour Party had a special and, as it proved, momentous conference to decide how to elect its Leader.

Some fashion notes from the conference at Wembley, the one where the trade union block voted for the predominance of trade union block votes. I was surprised that so many commentators seemed to be surprised. People who have a great deal of power are unlikely to use it in order to give themselves less power.

One felt that the block vote should have applied to the first ballot of the day, which was on whether smoking should be permitted. This would have meant that even if every single person in the hall, with the exception of Terry Duffy, Moss Evans, Clive Jenkins, Alan Fisher and David Basnett, had wanted a ban, and the five union leaders had fancied a fag, smoking would have been permitted by 3,667,000 votes to 3,533,000. There is the logic of the new democracy.

Back to fashion. Most Labour MPs, with a few exceptions, are absolutely middle-class. They dress in suits during the week. Most trade unionists are working class and wear working clothes of one kind or another during the week. When they go to a special conference they dress up properly, in suits, or brightly patterned sports jackets in manmade fibres, with matching tie and handkerchief sets. The MPs, however, pathetically anxious to ingratiate themselves, try to dress in the style they imagine is approved by the workers. So they appear in casual heather-mixture sports coats, open-neck shirts and corduroy slacks, with the kind of soft suede shoes that look as if they were made by their children at school. I saw one well-known QC wearing a bomber jacket. They all looked very silly, and it was quite clear that the workers felt their dress utterly unfitted to such an important occasion.

Mr Neville Sandelson, the well known kamikaze Labour MP who has been a founder-member of the Social Democratic Council, abandoned, I'm sorry to say, his plan to infuriate the delegates by turning up with a batch of smoked salmon sandwiches and a bottle of hock. He chickened out and had a catered lunch like everyone else. But when the manic Scotch chairman, Alex Kitson, attempted to throw out the press photographers, who had been annoying everyone by taking photographs for the press, Sandelson shouted, 'You can do that in Russia!' at the top of his voice, so attracting the wrathful stares of the many militants gathered around him.

A well-known Tory wet has come up with a marvellous time-saving plan which he plans to put shortly into action. He sits for a northern constituency, one of the many which swung Mrs Thatcher's way in 1979, and which is, no doubt regretting its folly as job after job disappears.

The MP says he is getting a printed form made for him on the usual 'strike out where not applicable' lines. It will read roughly: 'Dear – – –, It was with great regret that I learned of the closure of your factory/mill/plant/offices with the consequent loss of 100/200/300/400/500/1,000 jobs. I will/will not be able to attend your protest rally/march/delegation to Downing Street. If there is anything further which I can do to help, please let me know. I am, yours sincerely, – – – MP.

'This will save me hours a week,' he chortled.

Party Conferences exist in another world, displaced from the real one through a slight warp in space. For a start, many of the participants are in an alcoholic haze from the beginning of the conference until the end. They don't have to drink very much, merely to top up each morning with a pale ale or a gin and tonic. Sleep is a brief event, occurring haphazardly, and has no effect on the pleasant stupor. One well-known journalist could be seen in his usual position on the floor of the conference hotel lounge most evenings. Passing politicians would greet him as they stepped over him. At one Liberal conference the journalist hailed Lord Evans of Claughton.

'Ah, Gruff,' he cried, for that is the name to which his lordship answers, 'I wonder if you might have a Diary story for me. I find myself in need of a Diary story.'

Lord Evans always keen to oblige a friend, said that yes, he did have a story suitable for the paper's Diary column. The journalist waved a shorthand notebook at him and asked, 'Would you do me a favour and write it down in this, there's a good chap.'

The social life of a conference begins early, at breakfast time, when delegates, politicians and press toy unhappily with their fatty bacon and eggs, soggy toast, and thin beige-coloured coffee. They compare notes about the previous night's excesses, examining each other for redness of eye and whiteness of face. By 10.30 most people are feeling a little better, and it is time for the first drinkie of the day, to restore the alcohol level to par. Jimmy Durante used to say of teetotallers, 'Imagine waking up in the morning and knowing that's as good as you are going to feel all day.' Old conference hands wake up in the morning and know that's *exactly* how they are going to feel all day.

The need to attend the occasional debate and chat to the occasional politician can interfere with the smooth passage of the conference, though happily the proceedings are generally over at around 5 pm. The serious socializing begins at around 8, and continues until roughly 4 in the morning. Sensible seaside hotels keep efficient night porters at work serving miniatures of whisky to customers too much at ease to realize the prices they are being charged.

The story is told of Willie Whitelaw retiring to bed in the small hours each night of one Tory conference. His wife is alleged to have inquired why he needed to stay up so late, and he replied that he had been kept up by the press, always asking more questions. This line worked well until his wife came down for breakfast in a lift with two journalists, one of whom was moaning that 'Old Willie never stops. Kept us up till 3 last night, and I couldn't leave in case he said something important.'

The social fulcrum is the conference hotel, always the

Imperial in Blackpool and either the Grand or the Metropole in Brighton. These establishments keep out the riff-raff by charging grotesque prices for their drinks. This means that only Conservatives and people with expense accounts can go there. One reason they go is to be seen by the thousands of BBC personnel who criss-cross the lobby, ceaselessly looking for MPs and hacks to appear on radio programmes or even, prize of prizes, *Panorama*. No one has ever counted the number of BBC employees at a party conference: as well count the pebbles on Brighton beach. There is probably one for every three or four delegates.

The rooms in the conference hotel are usually occupied by party big-wigs, though inverted snobbery puts some of Labour's National Executive in little boarding houses. The Labour Treasurer, Norman Atkinson, likes to stay in one of these, where he can brew tea and his wife can iron his shirts. By contrast the Tory Treasurer, Mr Alistair McAlpine, has a magnificent suite in the Imperial, with a vast cocktail cabinet and velour hangings, so that it looks like a cross between a cheap Indian restaurant and a *fin de siècle* brothel.

After the final speeches the delegates rush for the trains home. By now there is a dangerous quantity of blood in their alcohol stream, and this has to be topped up in the buffet. It's easy for the delegates, since they have to attend only one conference a year. Some of us go to all three, more than 6 per cent of the working year. We have, and we need, the other 49 weeks to forget.

It is ironic indeed that it is Mrs Thatcher's suspicion of Mr Michael Heseltine, her Environment Secretary, which is doing Mr Heseltine so much good with his colleagues. After his conference speech this year, one found the bars at Blackpool crowded with junior ministers and MPs saying what an excellent speech it was, how Michael had finally proved himself, etc. etc. In past years they would have been wincing and cringing at the memory of that awful harangue: Rabble-Rouser to the Gentry.

Partly this is because reports are coming back from Cabinet that he is actually standing up to La Thatcher, daring to disagree with her on important issues like the trade unions and public spending cuts. It is reported that the Prime Minister has been heard to demand anxiously, 'Is Michael one of *us*?' Certainly, he seems keen to establish that he is not one of them.

But he does remain frightfully keen on himself. It is a convention at Tory conferences, for instance, that members of the Cabinet speak as if they were the head of a team of bright-eyed eager ministers, all pulling together in the common effort. But Heseltine says, '*I* have decided' and '*I* am going to ask Parliament,' even when it is quite clear that the real job will have to be done by people like John Stanley and Tom King who work under him.

A year or so ago, he made one of his famous rants to the conference, and for the rest of the day walked round in a kind of fog of congratulations. A very well known and senior broadcaster encountered him at a reception in the evening and remarked loudly, 'Michael, I thought that was the most appalling speech.'

'Thank you so very much, most kind of you,' Heseltine said.

Only a few minutes later did the words actually penetrate the miasma, and Heseltine was back wanting to know what the broadcaster had really meant.

One of the more pleasantly stupid traditions in the House of Commons can be seen when somebody wants to raise a point of order during a division. While a vote is on, the place is full of people milling around, so to attract the Speaker's attention the MP sits down and puts on a hat. Until recently any old headgear would do, a hanky or an order paper, but if the MP wished, he could go to the Serjeant at Arms' chair and have handed to him a battered old opera hat. The hat never quite stood up; if it ever achieved full erection, it would soon collapse on one side or the other. It gave a pleasantly raffish or drunken air to whoever wore it, so that he looked a little like an Edwardian reveller lurching down Piccadilly in the small hours. Mrs Renee Short recently used it; she was dressed in a brilliant mixture of colours, and the hat, half tumescent on her curly head, made her look so much like Harpo Marx that one expected her to signal the Speaker by pulling a motor horn out from under her jacket.

Mr George Cunningham, the MP for Islington who did so much to destroy the devolution bills, has not made it his life work to abolish the hat, but he has devoted a fair proportion of the past few weeks to it. Mr Cunningham believes that it is 'contrary to the dignity of this House and of every Member in it' to have to wear 'a comic old opera hat wrapped in a scruffy envelope'.

He was up against a recommendation from the important and influential procedure committee which had spent many hours pondering the problem of the hat. Faced with the choice of keeping it or abolishing it, they reached a compromise: they decided on two hats. The second one is now kept by the Speaker's chair. One wonders where they buy these things from. The Commons must be the last market for collapsible opera hats. One imagines some ancient and wizened hatter working from a small alleyway or mews in Bloomsbury, faced with rates, VAT demands and fuel bills, certain to close forever in weeks, when miraculously the Commons votes (as it did) by 194 votes to 103 to order another hat.

What makes the whole issue even more ludicrous is that the hat is not really part of some time-encrusted tradition. It dates from the eighteenth century when all members wore hats in the Chamber all the time.

When they rose to speak, they took off their hats. While they were sitting, as they would be for points of order during divisions, they kept their hats on. As the practice of wearing headgear in the Chamber died out, a special hat was provided for members to wear while seated for this particular purpose. So the silly object is really the result of a strange back-formation of tradition, as tourist villages sometimes invent colourful ceremonies to go with long-forgotten festivities.

Mr St John-Stevas, once Leader of the House, said that he was 'entirely detached in these matters; the only hat that I am interested in is a red one'. What can this mean? Perhaps he intends to take a job at Butlin's.

I gather that recently one of the young Foreign Office high-fliers rang Downing Street for an urgent conversation with another civil servant about a pressing matter. Three days previously Lord Carrington's office had sent a submission to Number Ten for their comments. What, he demanded of the somewhat starchy woman who answered the phone, were they doing about it? When was the FO going to get the reply? and to whom, he asked with icy courtesy, did he have the pleasure of speaking? 'The Prime Minister,' the woman replied. She then slammed the phone down.

As the Labour Party tears itself apart, it's fascinating to

watch the wrigglings and the contortions of those who are left behind, sadly flapping on the beach like so many tar-stained seabirds. They are, of course, in an awful quandary. Terrified of leaving the party and so perhaps destroying their political careers, they are equally petrified at the thought that the electors might equate them with the ghastly militants who are taking over chunks of the old Labour Party. (Actually, an interesting sociological development is that the real Lefties are now often very smoothly dressed; Stuart Holland MP looks like a prosperous executive and the ultra-lefty, Reg Race MP, whom I have seen sporting a smart sage-green leather blouson, might be the advertising manager of *Men In Vogue*.)

To protect themselves, those left behind in the party have developed a more rhetorical trick which one hears more and more often. It could be called the ATWIS syndrome, ATWIS being almost the acronym for And That's Why I'm A Socialist. It is used as the emphasis, the exclamation mark at the end of virtually any declaration of principle or policy, for example, 'I happen to believe there are more important things in life than colour TVs, wall-to-wall carpeting and digital watches, things called equality and justice. And that's why I'm a Socialist!' The phrase can be used the other way round, viz. 'I happen to believe that there's one thing which is just a bit more important than equality for the sake of equality – something called prosperity. ATWIS!'

The phrase, guaranteed to thrill the collective heart of any Labour Party audience, can be applied to any philosophy from Left to Right. 'I happen to believe in something called human enterprise, the right of people to seek their fortunes without interference from the state. ATWIS!'

Alternatively, 'I happen to believe in the inevitability of the class struggle, the overthrow of the corrupt bourgeois system, and the wholesale extermination of the kulaks. ATWIS!'

In any event, we shall be hearing a great deal more of ATWIS in the months to come. My advice is to suspect anyone who uses it and to examine what they say with great care. They are certainly trying to burke the issues.

Now and again, the Labour Party presents a comedy revue.

Labour got the idea from the Tories, who put on every year a revue attacking the Labour Party. They thought this an excellent plan, and so most years they put on their own revue attacking the Labour Party. There is the odd joke against the Tories ('I asked Sir Keith what he'd have to drink and he said, "Oh, the usual, a Rhesus Negative with ice and lemon." ') but the real pleasure comes from getting stuck into Tony Benn, Harold Wilson, Roy Hattersley and the rest of the comrades. I like very much the representative of the Audience's Union ('The management promised that the first half would last only 50 minutes. We are now in a 55-minute situation, and therefore I have negotiated a seventeen-minute interval. Ignore the so-called warning bell; this is a management ploy...') and the haunting closing number: 'If you were the only Shirl in the world, and I were the only Woy.'

One of the best gags was to be heard not on stage but in the bar afterwards: 'That Jim Prior; he's so wet that if you added him to a tub of Bachelor's Pot Noodle you could feed the unemployed for a week.'

An unnerving story reached me indirectly from our popular, genial Home Secretary, Mr Whitelaw. He told it to his many chums shortly after the SAS successfully raided the Iranian Embassy in London.

Willie was receiving a formal visit from his opposite number in West Germany, the Minister of the Interior. This Teutonic statesman said that the one thing in Britain he wanted to see above all else was the SAS, so in conditions of great secrety he and Willie were taken to Hereford where the regiment gets up to its various distasteful practices, lying in vats of fresh offal, and so forth.

After they had been shown round, the two men were told by the senior officer that they would now be given a demonstration of the SAS's amazing skills. They were taken alone, into a small room and told that whatever happened they were not to panic. Indeed, under no circumstances should they move even a muscle. The officer then left the room.

The two men stood against the wall, more than a shade apprehensive. Suddenly the door burst open. Several men in balaclavas rushed into the room and instantaneously began firing machine guns – apparently straight at the ministers' heads. The German, I gather, almost collapsed with horror. When, seconds later, the firing stopped they turned round and saw that the soldiers had drilled a perfectly neat pattern of holes into the wall around their heads, two inverted 'U's', as close fitting as a giantess's bra.

Willie said subsequently that what gave him the greatest chill was the thought, had things gone terribly wrong, of the phone call he would have had to make to Margaret Thatcher telling her of the phone call she would have to make to Helmut Schmidt.

Meanwhile, Westminster is now full of moles spotting the latest 'Willieisms', those death-defying logical leaps for which the Home Secretary is famous. Recently he was making a statement about the escape of IRA man Gerald Tuite and the subsequent transfer of the prison governor. With the air of one shouldering the burdens of the world, Willie said, 'I, of course, accept responsibility. But then, if

I accepted responsibility for everything, I would not last long in this job.'

There are serious doubts at Westminster about just how much more Sir Keith Joseph can take. People have been predicting for at least fifteen years to my knowledge that he is about to crack up, and he never has. But something awesome must surely be about to happen.

A Tory MP tells me that recently he went into one of the 'division' or voting lobbies which are, in fact, wide, book-lined corridors. He wanted a piece of paper to scribble a note upon.

Then he noticed that it was not quite deserted. Sir Keith was standing there, very gently but rhythmically banging his head against the wall.

Recently he attended a political meeting somewhere in the Midlands. A member of the audience tells me that while the introductory remarks were being made and the first, preliminary, speakers were on their feet, Sir Keith spent the entire time with his leg hoist over his knee first loosening, then tying, then untying, then knotting again, his shoelaces. He did it literally dozens of times before his turn came to speak.

Not long ago a group of journalists took him to eat at a very expensive London restaurant indeed, the kind where the menus come on scrolls of parchment the size of billboards. The hacks were choosing between oysters and smoked salmon, followed by lobster or pheasant or porterhouse steaks, when the waiter approached and asked the Secretary of State for Industry what he would like. Sir Keith's brow knitted, he paused, then said, 'I think I'll just have a piece of cake.' After a short but meaningful silence, the waiter asked what type of cake he would like. 'I think, British Rail cake,' said Sir Keith, and as the Fourth Estate chomped through their Lucullan troughs, he ate a piece of fruit and nut cake as served in plastic packets on trains.

At another lunch, this time given by businessmen, each time the conversation became too much for him, he would get up from the table and march up and down the room, slapping his forehead. I mentioned this to a colleague of Sir Keith's. 'Oh that's nothing,' he said, 'He does it in Cabinet too. Sometimes he even leaves the room to do it.'

The House of Commons can be simultaneously a very cruel and a very kindly place. Any MP who falls foul of the press or suffers some awful personal affliction can be assured of loyal support from his colleagues on both sides, a slap on the back, a sympathetic note, a large brandy. Take the events surrounding Mr Allan Roberts, the Labour MP for Bootle, whose curious adventures in a homosexual nightclub in Berlin formed such a large part of the political reportage in the *News of the World*.

If he had turned up at the House, Roberts would have found just how kind and thoughtful MPs can be to somebody in trouble. However, he did not. His name headed the list for those to ask the Prime Minister a question, the position all MPs crave and some never manage in a lifetime at Westminster. But when the Speaker called his name, Roberts was not there, and the Commons showed its snarl.

'Where izzee?' the Tories shouted, and the answers came back 'Gone walkies!', 'With the whips again' and 'He's tied up elsewhere!' All good smutty schoolboy fun, but according to their peculiar code, none of it would have been said in his presence.

I make no apology for stealing a splendid item from *Labour Weekly* which that paper in turn stole from Kelvingrove Labour Party in Glasgow. The Scots provided, in their annual report, a glossary of terms used in the party as a guide to newcomers. This is invaluable; in fact there is sufficient detail here for the Berlitz people to set up classes. 'I'm willing to stand as Secretary' means 'I want to be the MP'. The line 'This is really quite uncontroversial, comrades' means 'We are setting up a Trotskyist front organization'. 'Comrades, we meet at a time of growing

141

crisis in the Labour Party/Government/trade unions/capitalist system' means 'I'm a Trotskyist'.

'Comrades, I have spoken for long enough' means 'I've forgotten what I was about to say'; 'I think the most important thing to have come out of this discussion is. . .' means 'I am now going to repeat what I said earlier'. *Labour Weekly* adds some examples of its own: 'Speaking as a member of the working classes' means 'I'm middle class/in full-time education'. 'We are now in a classless society' means 'As a member of the ruling class'. 'We must become a classless society' means 'I would like to join the ruling class'.

Naturally, the Tories have their equivalent, and I have been pondering on one or two of them. 'We all have the most tremendous admiration for the job Margaret Thatcher is doing. . .' means 'I cannot stand the old cow and am about to criticize her as viciously as I dare'. 'Nobody could describe me as a racialist' means 'I am a racialist'. 'Speaking as a trade unionist' means 'Speaking as a member of an exclusive professional association designed to screw the general public' and, a common formulation at party conferences, 'If being working class means being a worker, then, fellow Conservatives, I am working class!' equals 'I have a cushy job in the City which involves turning up from 11 to 4 with a three-hour break for lunch'. 'No one can doubt the sincerity of those Conservatives who are calling for capital punishment in secondary schools' means 'Personally I would boil the lot of them in smoking Mazola'.

I went to Oldham to see the enjoyable play by Labour MP Joe Ashton, *A Majority of One*. It's all about life in the Whips' office during a day of crucial votes for the last Government. Ashton is no great dramatist, but he has caught perfectly the crackling atmosphere of the Labour Whips' office, a cross between an NCOs' mess and a used car showroom.

One story he hasn't included was about the late Joe

Harper, who used to be MP for Pontefract. Among their duties, Whips have to count MPs voting as they walk past the clerks, shouting, '278, 279,' and so forth as they go past. Another more unpleasant duty, when the voting is close, is to tour round the sick and maimed who are brought in when pairing arrangements have been banned. These people don't need to walk past the clerks, but they must be physically present in the Palace for their vote to count.

One such was Mr Leslie Spriggs, the MP for St Helens, who had had a heart attack. Against all doctors' advice he had been brought to the Commons in the back of an ambulance, where he lay totally unconscious, hooked up to various life support systems and electronic recording machines. Harper had the gruesome job of visiting all the diseased and moribund persons to prove to a Tory Whip that they were actually present. He wrenched open the back door of Sprigg's ambulance and the Tory peered in. After a moment he said suspicously, 'How do I know he's still alive?'

'Whaddyamean, how do you know he's alive?' shouted Harper angrily. A meaty miner's fist shot out and punched a red button attached to a silent TV monitor. Suddenly there was a loud 'bleep' and a bright green arc travelled swiftly across the screen. 'There you are, 280!' Harper said with satisfaction.

The only good news from this unsavoury tale of democracy in action is that Mr Spriggs made a complete recovery.

The Labour Party introduces its party political broadcasts on a shoestring. A great deal less time and money goes into them than into, say, a single day's *Jackanory*. The camera crew do the work for a pork pie and a pint, and the filming is over in one day. If a minister or a backbencher is to do the commentary, or 'voice-over', then he must make his way to London's vice-ridden Soho where, if he is astute and fortunate, he may find the tiny attic where the producer is putting the final touches to the film.

One such MP, clutching a script full of references to unemployment and marginal income tax rates, was walking through Soho trying to find this minute and dingy cutting room. He was peering carefully at the small name-plates and plaques at each door with their legends 'Annie, Model' and 'Karen, French Lessons' when a policeman recognized him and stopped.

'Excuse me, sir, may I help you?' he asked with heavy Ealing-comedy style irony.

'Ah yes, you see officer. I'm making a party political broadcast for the Labour Party. . .' the crouching legislator said.

'Blimey,' said the policeman, 'that's the first time I've ever heard that one.'

In 1981 Sir Peter Hayman was named as a member of the 'Paedophile Information Exchange':

The Geoffrey Dickens saga continues to unfold, like successive scenes in some awful Grand Guignol production, each more grisly than the last. Mr Dickens is the fat Tory MP for Huddersfield who first named the wretched Sir Peter Hayman on the Commons order paper. Sir Peter and his disgusting fantasies appear to have evaporated from the public mind, to be replaced by the huge and sweating figure of Dickens whose own love life seems by contrast to be merely a grotesque version of our own. There may be an awful lot of them, but at least they're all over 21.

The most bizarre suggestion of all is that there should be an inquiry into the source of Mr Dickens's leak. By now every single person at Westminster knows who passed on Hayman's name. It was a journalist whose identity I cannot reveal, but who is thought to be a member of the Draught Guinness Information Exchange. This journalist had made several attempts to persuade an MP – any MP

– to name Sir Peter, and Dickens was the only one who took the bait.

At this stage Dickens did not even know what paedophiles actually did, and had to have it explained to him. For some time he kept mispronouncing the word 'Fido pills' as if they were vitamin drops for dogs.

When he held a press conference to announce that he had left his wife for another woman, he begged the assembled hacks not to ring home and ask what his wife felt.

'I haven't had the time to tell her yet,' he explained, demonstrating once again his limitless consideration. After the conference ended, he went to the phone and rang home, only to find the line engaged. The *Daily Star* was already on to Mrs Dickens, breaking the news to her.

Most Tory MPs now treat Dickens as if he were the club leper, or had been caught cheating at cards. Every time he opens his mouth a collection of tedious and pompous windbags make loud baying noises. The British upper classes have always been endlessly tolerant of sexual excess, whereas working-class people like Mr Dickens find it shocking – even more shocking than, say, wearing brown shoes with a blue suit.

I see that Lord Avebury, the famous Liberal peer and do-gooder (what is wrong with do-gooders? Why is it a term of abuse? Would people prefer do-badders?) has been complaining about MPs' drinking habits. He says it is wrong for the bars at Westminster to stay open for as long as the House is sitting. In a Lords debate Avebury, the former Eric Lubbock, remarked, 'It is unthinkable that Fords of Dagenham should have a night bar, so if workers felt thirsty they could slip away for a few pints.'

What nonsense! For one thing the employees at Dagenham do not have to work shifts up to 16 hours long, and when they are present there is generally some work for them to do. If MPs did not have bars in which to while away the long night watches, they would only be making nuisances of themselves, going up to the Chamber, making speeches and legislating. They are much better off sitting quietly in front of a pint, where we can keep an eye on them and they can do nobody any harm.

But Lord Avebury's remarks set me thinking about the long tradition of booze in the Commons. There was the late Sir Waldron Smithers, MP for Orpington, whose acquaintanceship with John Barleycorn was closer than that of many an MP with his pair. Once the Speaker asked which day a Bill was to get its second reading and the Clerk made the formal reply, 'Friday October 5th, Sir!' The silence was broken by the delighted voice of Sir Waldron: 'Thash my birthday!'

The late Sir Walter Bromley-Davenport, Member for Knutsford and briefly a Government Whip, once kicked a Tory backbencher *upstairs* while in his cups. Churchill, no slouch with the brandy glass himself, was obliged to sack Sir Walter, replacing him with the more abstemious young member for Bexleyheath, one Lt-Col Edward Heath.

In more recent times, Lord George-Brown was not averse to the occasional — even the more-than-occasional — gin and tonic while standing in for Harold Wilson as Prime Minister. Mr Whitelaw, our genial Home Secretary, is not loth to sip a small scotch or, if strongly pressed, a large one. Mrs Thatcher will take a drop of malt while working late on a speech and even the present Speaker, a lifelong abstainer, nowadays occasionally takes a modest libation before retiring.

To those who believe in the absurd idea that somehow this country would be better governed if there were not so much liquor flowing through the House of Commons, I would point out that the most rigidly teetotal Member of Parliament, a man whose knowledge of booze is so limited that when pouring a scotch for someone else he will fill a brimming tumbler with the stuff at four in the afternoon, is Mr Tony Benn.

What a charming man Lord Home is! He was recently travelling on a train between Edinburgh and London when he was recognized by a middle-aged woman who was with her husband.

'Ooh,' she said, 'it's Sir Alec Douglas-Home, isn't it? How marvellous to see you. I've always admired you and I tell my husband that the greatest tragedy of British life is that you never became Prime Minister!'

Sir Alec smiled with his famous, faultless, diffident politeness, then murmured, 'Thank you so very much. As a matter of fact I was Prime Minister – but only for a very short time.'

A lot of his friends – and there are very many – are wondering why Michael Foot is such a rotten performer on television. It's not as if he hasn't had much practice; indeed, back in the days of Muffin the Mule, the Grove Family, and the potter's wheel which whizzed round during the lengthy gaps between programmes, when the few people who watched TV did so either on tiny little Bakelite sets or else vast mahogany jobs with sliding doors tricked out to look like Georgian cocktail cabinets – back in those days Michael Foot was barely off the screens.

That, of course, was when politicians were not expected to woo the electorate by appearing as relaxed as Val Doonican on Valium. There was none of this nonsense about sitting in chintzy armchairs, saying 'y'know' every second sentence and blowing enough tobacco smoke to provide cover for an aircraft carrier leaving Scapa Flow. Politicians were expected to do what they did best – abuse each other. No one else would do it for them. Interviewers had the task of painlessly extracting from whoever they sat opposite exactly what they wanted to say. Before the advent of Robin Day they were scarcely ever challenged. After they had finished, the interviewer would say, with the air of a curate thanking the Archbishop, 'Thank you, sir, for coming to the studio to explain your bill to the viewers.'

In this reverential atmosphere it is small wonder that the *In The News* programme, launched in 1949 by Edgar

Lustgarten, was such a success. The regular panel of four, chaired by the sinister mystery writer, was Foot, Robert Boothby, A. J. P. Taylor, and a now forgotten Tory MP called W. J. Brown. They used to discuss topical issues and abuse all about them. Foot's saying, delivered while white with passion, 'You're talking absolute tripe, and you know it,' almost became a national catch-phrase. What was more, since he and Boothby were mavericks with scant regard for the leaders of their own parties, they used to direct their fiercest and most astringent attacks at those who were nominally on their own sides. In the end the heads of both party machines went along to complain to the BBC, which reacted with the stiff resolve we have come to associate with it in all its tussles with politicians. It surrendered immediately. Tedious placemen who could be guaranteed to trot out the party line on all issues were substituted for the original panel and the programme died an obscure and unlamented death in 1954.

In these days of relaxed and intimate chats between politician and interviewer Foot is less at home. His natural diffidence, which so delights his friends, makes him look fairly shifty, as if he is unwilling to answer the questions. The effect is heightened by his nervousness; occasionally the camera pans back to reveal a nervous foot tapping rhythmically against a chair leg. His anxiety to address himself to all sections of the Labour Party prevents him from addressing himself to the electorate, which must occasionally feel like an onlooker in some obscure family quarrel.

Foot can have the consolation, however, of knowing that he is unlikely to create so disastrous an effect as that produced by his hero, Aneurin Bevan. Bevan, who in 1959 was Labour's Deputy Leader, had always refused to appear on a party political broadcast. He felt correctly that his home was on the public platform. For the 1959 election, however, he was persuaded to change his mind and agreed to appear on condition that the broadcast took the form of an interview. The interviewer he chose was his old friend, Tom Driberg, not the wisest selection he could have made.

Driberg opened with some anodyne question, on the lines of: 'What do you think about the present political situation?' and Bevan began talking, or rather began making a speech. His speech lasted for exactly 14½ minutes. At this point the studio manager signalled to Driberg to end the programme. Driberg said, 'So that's what you think?', Bevan replied 'Yes,' and the interview was over.

Engaged in some political research the other day, I began to notice how rarely people had actually said what people think they said. Take jokes. If you were to ask a dozen friends which was Sir Winston Churchill's wittiest crack, I'd guess most would mention his quickfire riposte to Lady Astor, who once accused him of being drunk. 'And you, madam, are ugly. But I shall be sober in the morning.' Except that there is no evidence whatever that Churchill made this reply to Lady Astor or to any other woman. Someone is supposed to have remarked to Lord Balogh

(or Lord Kaldor) that Lord Kaldor (or Lord Balogh) was his own worst enemy. 'Not while I'm alive,' the other is alleged to have replied, as perhaps he did, except that the identical story is told of Bevan and Gaitskell, George Brown and Harold Wilson, Giscard and Chirac, and almost any other well known pair of rivals you can think of.

But jokes are part of the national folklore. What's surprising is the way that perfectly ordinary, serious, phrases and epigrams have been changed, twisted and misattributed. Frequently, politicians get the credit for other people's clever remarks. In July 1961, Hardiman Scott, the BBC political pundit, asked Selwyn Lloyd on *Radio Newsreel* if he was proposing something called a 'wage freeze'; Lloyd seized gratefully on the phrase and had it pinned to his name ever after.

John Pardoe never suggested that the Liberal Party needed 'a bit of a bastard' to lead it, though the general belief that he had might have helped lose him the election. A reporter asked him if he thought that's what the party required, and he agreed. In 1955, a Press Association reporter interviewed Rab Butler at Heathrow airport about the Prime Minister, Sir Anthony Eden.

'Would you say this is the best Prime Minister we have?' the reporter inquired. Butler paused for a moment, then said, 'Yes.' Not only is the saying now attributed to him, but it is presented as an indication of his wit, acumen, and skilful ability to mean far more than he says.

Ted Heath at no time said that he could cut prices 'at a stroke'. In the 1970 election, he spoke to a press conference. As the hacks assembled they were presented with the daily hand-out of news, comments and straight lies which the parties produce at poll times. That day's press release contained a long list of anti-inflation measures, and added, 'This would, at a stroke, reduce the rise in prices.' Heath didn't use the words, and probably did not know they were in the hand-out.

He did say 'the unacceptable face of capitalism,' but he

didn't intend to. Heath is short sighted, but usually too vain to wear glasses. Commenting on the Lonrho scandal in the House, he read from a script provided for him by Number Ten. But he couldn't quite make out the words typed on the page: 'This is an unpleasant and unacceptable facet of capitalism' – a far less memorable phrasing.

James Callaghan did not say 'Crisis? What crisis?' when he returned from the Guadeloupe summit of world leaders in January 1979. The headline appeared in the *Sun*, and caught the country's angered imagination much better than his actual words, 'I see no signs of mounting crisis,' would have done.

Harold Wilson did say 'the pound in your pocket,' in a misguided attempt to explain that goods in the shops would not immediately rise by the percentage by which the pound had just been devalued. But he never used the phrase 'a bonfire of controls' in the Attlee Government's period of office. The words 'a bonfire' and 'of controls' came in quite dissimilar sections of two separate speeches, and were coupled together by others, some time later. Nor, in 1963, did he talk about 'the white heat of technology,' though admittedly that was the gist of what he meant. In a speech in October, he addressed himself to the scientific revolution, and later on heralded 'the white heat of this revolution'.

Two of the most intriguing and often quoted remarks of the last quarter-century were nearly right. In July 1949, Nye Bevan said, 'No attempt at ethical or social education can eradicate from my heart a deep burning hatred for the Tory Party . . . so far as I am concerned, they are lower than vermin.' The difference is admittedly subtle, even altogether academic, but it is not exactly the same thing as claiming that people who vote Conservative are vermin – though from the way the speech was taken up, it would be hard to tell the difference.

In July 1957, Harold Macmillan (one of the three former Prime Ministers still alive who is still plain 'mister') addressed a Conservative rally in Bedford.

'Let us be frank about it,' he said. 'Most of our people have never had it so good.' 'The wind of change', 'Little local difficulties', he did say, but the exact words, 'You've never had it so good,' never passed his lips.

I ran into a senior member of the Government the other day who told me, with great glee, a splendid story about Lord Longford. His Lordship was walking through Soho, discussing with a friend the workings of the Indecent Displays Bill, due to come up to the House of Lords any day. (Incidentally, I gather that the powerful Whitehouse lobby has dropped its idea of trying to get the bill extended to cover the inside of dirty shops as well as the outside. They are afraid that they might lose the whole bill if they do. In any case, I don't see how you can have a sex shop without filthy objects on display somewhere. It would be like those expensive wine merchants where you choose from a catalogue, and the tail-coated assistant brings the bottle up from the cellar. 'Certainly, sir, I can recommend the Japanese tickler with confidence. . .')

Anyhow, Longford passed a shop that had, months ago, a window crammed with full-colour thighs, bosoms, buttocks and whips. Now it is covered in discreet black glass. 'You see,' said Longford, 'my work has not been in vain!' His friend did not have the heart to point out that the reason for this change was that the shop had been converted to a massage parlour, featuring exotic forms of muscular relaxation.

I've been fascinated to read a recent number of *Tory Action*, the magazine published by the right-wing ginger group of the same name. Just as the far Left has its own private jargon, a sort of ritualized sub-Trotsky at five removes, so the Right copies its style slavishly from the American ultra groups. Principally this means italicizing whole phrases, generally ones which are either particularly abusive or else have a stiff, old-fashioned ring. Mrs Thatcher, for example, is encouraged to 'emulate the *staunch spirit* of men like Julian Amery', a hero figure of the Right who is regarded with something less than admiration by most of his colleagues. Because of the strong American influence, transatlantic phrases creep in with and jostle alongside the circumlocutions of the club bore. Mr Heseltine is taken to pieces for sending rates *'through the roof'*. It goes on: 'Mrs Thatcher is thinking about doing something about this. *Just don't hold your breath while she does.'*

Tory Action threatens big trouble at party conferences, especially over the immigration debate which is usually, in the tradition of Tory conferences, a fix. *'We have taken an initiative that may wipe a few smiles off faces,'* the editor writes, though the force of this threat is muted by a later paragraph. 'We hope that the chairman will be a bit more gracious than Sir Charles Johnson, who sent us a very rude letter last year when we denounced his manipulation of the motions.' One can't be terribly worried about their ruthless determination if they get upset by a rude letter.

Just as one is always made faintly dizzy by people who think that Tony Benn is too right-wing, so one's brain begins to spin when one realizes that these people regard Mrs Thatcher as a left-wing menace. '"The Fuehrerin is always right, even when she is wrong" is exactly what is *not* required' they write.

Tory Action casts a judicious eye over foreign affairs as well as domestic issues. On the Commonwealth, they muse thoughtfully: 'If there have been two more appalling individuals than *Pierre Trudeau* and *Gough Whitlam*, it is difficult to imagine who they can be (unless it is their wives).' *Tory Action* answers its own question a page or so later. The Foreign Office, it says dramatically, is 'a body rooted in treason and dishonour'. But my favourite section of the whole paper, available from PO Box 850, London W14, is the signing off. These people actually believe that the Tolpuddle Martyrs were justly sentenced. 'We note that the law which got (them) deported has now been

153

repealed – although now is probably the time we would do with it most.'

I once knew a British ultra-right-winger (like many of them, he was of Irish descent) who quite seriously argues for the return of the Rotten Boroughs system. That's what I like about our loony Right, their endearingly screwy sense of history.

I've been reading through a fascinating booklet written by Mr Chris Mullin, who is one of Mr Tony Benn's most enthusiastic henchman, a sort of Boswell on lobby terms. It is called *How to Select or Reselect your MP*; in other words it is a do-it-yourself guide to getting rid of your MP. Mr Mullin is an accomplished journalist, so the booklet is admirably written, and an entertaining read. If I were a Labour MP, it would send chills the length of my spine.

As always with the Left, it deals simply enough with the curious fact that the electorate is held to have voted Tory in 1970 and 1979 because Labour was not Left-wing enough. You may find this baffling, and consider that people did not choose Mrs Thatcher as a roundabout way of saying they really wanted Tony Benn.

However you would be wrong. In 1970 party workers were so fed up with Harold Wilson's policies, the result was 'a haemorrhage of members out of the Party and defeat in the general election'. In 1974–9, the pamphlet says quite erroneously: 'The government ended up doing a sordid little deal with the Ulster Unionists, for the purpose of keeping the backsides of Ministers in official limousines for another few months.' In fact there was no deal with the Unionists, and the government was motivated by the impeccably socialist ideal of keeping Mrs Thatcher out. But of course a Labour win in 1979 would have kept the Benn campaign in abeyance for a few years more.

The leaflet describes some of the ways to keep your MP in line. He must always ask permission of his local Party workers before doing anything. If there is no time for a full Party meeting, he must phone round the principal

154

offices. Generously, Mr Mullin says that having instructed your MP to vote against a Labour government, you must back him up. 'Accountability is a two-way process,' he says.

There follows a handy guide for giving the wretched chap the old heave-ho. Sometimes an MP is sufficiently popular for his party to want him to continue unopposed. 'This pressure should be resisted at all costs.' When you ask him questions, you should keep a careful note of the answers 'for use against the day when promises have to be translated into practice'. Get lots and lots of candidates against the fellow. 'Only the fixers have anything to fear from a large field.' It concludes: 'Labour MPs have no rights more or less than the ordinary card-carrying Party members. They are simply the Party members to whom has fallen the honour of giving practical expression to the ideals of the Labour Movement.' Well, actually, that is a bit of a fib. However fortunate they are in being chosen as candidates by Mr Mullin and his pals, MPs are elected by twenty or thirty thousand ordinary voters, for the sole purpose of representing them. Its a fascinating insight into the Benn campaign that not once in the entire booklet is there the slightest mention of the voters, or the least little hint that they have rights, just as much as Labour Party activists.

So rarely does this column gets its forecasts right, that it's worth reprinting these predictions. They appeared three months before Mrs Thatcher's September 1981 Cabinet changes. Their accuracy is less a testimony to investigative brilliance than to the way Mrs Thatcher makes public her (many) dissatisfactions with the Ministers she appoints.

Soon, according to many of the Conservative MPs you meet, it will be time for another Cabinet re-shuffle. 'Reshuffle' was actually the right kind of word for what previous Prime Ministers did; it conveys exactly the sense of slow deliberate movement. It implies that those who lost one job found themselves appointed to another, with perhaps only one dropping off the edge. The entire operation was like musical chairs played to Handel's *Largo*.

But Mrs Thatcher's Cabinet changes have a quite different style. They remind me more of those little competitions in the *Generation Game*. Isla and Larry stand respectfully over some acknowledged expert in the field of cake-icing or napkin-folding or macramé-eating. A sudden slice here, a swift incision there, the detritus pushed to the side, and within fifteen seconds a beautifully finished something-or-other. The contestants attempt the same movements but end up with an amusingly botched job, to the delight of the audience.

Mrs Thatcher's next assault on her Cabinet will be much the same; quick and surgical, the movements of the knife hardly visible. Around Westminster, Tory MPs are even now filling in the backs of their diaries and notebooks with their predictions of where each precise stroke will cut. They have become obsessive about the lightest word of her Parliamentary Private Secretary, Mr Ian Gow, who, it is assumed, is always acting as a messenger on her behalf. 'He came up to me last night,' one Tory mused to me, 'and said he thought it looked like rain. Do you think that means I might get Environment?' If Gow said, 'I can never remember how many "s's" in "assess", that would mean you were in line for Education; if he asks you for the loan of your lighter, that indicated Energy. 'Pass the milk,' means Agriculture, and so on.

So who will be sliced off from the Cabinet and allowed to fall on to the floor? Step forward (as Crossbencher in the *Sunday Express* might say) Mr Mark Carlisle. Rescued as Education Secretary last time because of the attacks on him by Mr Neil Kinnock, his Labour opposite number, he surely cannot last much longer. Furthermore, Mr Carlisle has not been sufficiently unpopular with the teaching profession, partly because he has fought against the cuts imposed on him. This will not do. Back in the Heath Government, it was the job of the Education Secretary to be positively hated by the profession.

Many Tories now believe that she will get rid of Sir Ian Gilmour, the deputy Foreign Secretary, and one of the most delightful men in the Cabinet. Sir Ian still has a powerful protector, his boss Lord Carrington, and he has not made the mistake of delivering any more disloyal speeches. I recently predicted that the sacking of Mr St John-Stevas would not bring Sir Ian quietly to heel. I was wrong. It appears to have had exactly that effect.

Some say she would like to get rid of the incredibly tall Mr David Howell, the Energy Secretary. He looks like one of those children's cartoons in which characters are run over by steam rollers. Any moment you expect the frame to jerk and Mr Howell to snap back to a normal shape.

She has a terrible problem of what to do with Sir Keith Joseph. Sir Keith's threatened breakdown has, like Billy Bunter's postal order, been expected, but has failed to turn up for many years. Yet it is clear that he cannot last much longer as Secretary for Industry. Frankly, Sir Keith, though a man of great intelligence and even attractiveness, is not up to the job of being a Minister. From the days when he decided on high-rise blocks for council tenants, from the re-organization of the Health Service, he has been making terrible mistakes. He invariably apologizes to us all, and, unlike most political apologists, he is clearly sincere. But while he thus shrives himself and rests at peace with his soul, the rest of us have to live with his ghastly bishes.

What she ought to do is have a special 'Think-Tank' of Ministers in the Cabinet who can sit there being brainy but wouldn't be allowed to get their cack-handed mitts on our day-to-day lives. Sir Keith could join Mr Howell and Lord Hailsham, who is, I fear, also now past it. They could sit at one end of the table and fidget, while the rest got on with the job.

And who will be promoted? Mr Nigel Lawson, 'Niglet'

157

to his enemies, is the Financial Secretary to the Treasury, and cannot be kept outside the Cabinet much longer. He is living proof that it is better to have 338 Conservative MPs against you and the Prime Minister on your side, than to be loved by the 338 and not by her.

Watch out for her old side-kick Norman Tebbit, the boot boy of the Tory Right, who once shouted to the late Tom Litterick, 'Why don't you have another heart attack?' As an Industry Minister Mr Tebbit (who is, in reality, rather nice) has been an unexpected success. So has her old PPS John Stanley, at Housing, and the agreeable Mr Tom King, in Local Government. Watch out too for smooth, elegant grammar-school bred (but you'd hardly notice) Cecil Parkinson of Trade. He has been touring the world stitching up arms deals and the like with shady Third World potentates. When Mrs Thatcher pays a well-publicized visit to these same countries a few months later, she is able to claim the sale as a personal triumph. Mr Parkinson's discreet loyalty will find its reward.

In June 1981, Tony Benn went into hospital to be treated for Guillame-Baire syndrome.

One of the most engaging features of the House of Commons is the way that, unlike grouse shooting, there is no close season for political feuding. Kicking a man when he is down is not only thought legitimate; it is regarded as quite the best time for the boot to thud in. If a chap is ill and in hospital, then so much the better. For example, no sooner had Tony Benn gone in than one of his Left-wing colleagues grumbled: 'That's the first time I've heard of a brain specialist treating a pain in the arse.'

I was chatting the other day to a Labour MP who had attended a plush dinner in London for Vice-President George Bush. At the end Bush had said that he had time to answer four questions. Denis Healey then spoke up and managed to ask all four. At one point he said of one country, El Salvador, Guatemala, or perhaps Britain, that the US had 'got them by the genitals'. My informant tells me: 'Denis would have used the usual shorter word, if he hadn't had sitting next to him the Archbishop of Canterbury.'

In July 1981, the column visited the historic Warrington by-election, where the SDP scored its famous Phyrric defeat. As usual, the final analysis was mistaken.

The Social Democrats have been ruthlessly efficient at Warrington, where by polling day they expect to have canvassed every voter in the constituency once and all the doubtful ones twice. This is a remarkable feat for a new party, but with dozens of volunteers pouring in every day, not a difficult one. They have an American-style manner of paying attention to the little irrelevant details; for example they have one of those elaborate phones with buttons all over it. The base is white, the body blue and the handset red – the party colours.

I toured round a cake factory with Roy Jenkins. The firm was called Memory Lane, and its trademark was a sort of sepia-style picture of a Victorian family, evoking a by-gone era of Empire, security and respect for one's betters, a little like Mr Jenkins himself.

The cakes themselves were made from the finest traditional ingredients; Spray Dried Skimmed Milk Powder, Fat Reduced Cocoa Powder, and Malto Dextrin Sweetener, just like granny used to use. Outside the plant vast juggernauts were being loaded with Angel Layers, Strawberry Roules and Orange/Lemon Cupcakes, ready for the long haul down Memory Motorway to the supermarkets. Inside, oddly enough, the cakes were actually hand-made, or at least hand-finished. Nice Northern ladies dabbed

ROY JENKINS

whirls on the walnut slices, younger women actually hand-rolled each Swiss roll, and one plump lady almost fell into a vat of gungey white stuff which she loaded into a hopper for the Angel Layers. Mr Jenkins enjoyed himself greatly, occasionally mistaking people's friendliness for an intention to vote SDP. The public's courtesy to politicians always surprises me, and, indeed, them.

'I hope you will support us,' he would say, and they would reply, 'Oh yes.' This doesn't mean 'I'll vote for you' but is, rather, a general expression of goodwill and friendliness to a stranger.

Mr and Mrs Jenkins, and the small train of hacks they took round with them, were dressed in white with starched peaked caps, concealing everything except our faces.

'Is that Michael Foot with you?' one woman asked, peering at a hack. 'No, that is the political correspondent of the *Sunday People*,' Mr Jenkins replied, 'he's causing some confusion here' – as if the reporter should have put on a red nose and false beard so as to avoid being mistaken for Michael Foot. He is shamelessly flattering: 'I'm afraid those jam tarts wouldn't be any good for me,' he said, patting his stomach, 'but you can eat without getting fat' – to a woman whose figure suggested that she ate jam tarts for breakfast, lunch and tea. Mr Jenkins will, I fear, be the latest in a long line of politicians who imagine that because he was not actually pelted with Battenburg Slices that he will receive the public's support.

I asked a prominent Liberal MP how he and his Party were getting on with Dr David Owen, one fourth of the SDP leadership, or 'quartermaster' as he might be termed. 'Marvellously,' he told me. 'You see, he's frightfully rude and arrogant to all his colleagues. We used to think it was just us, and we resented it like mad. Now we see him do it to them, and we don't mind a bit.'

I gather that, contrary to general belief, Denis Thatcher detested his depiction in the farce *Anyone for Denis?*. He and his wife (who also found it pretty distasteful) had to sit through the performance smiling and were obliged to entertain the cast at Downing Street afterwards because it was all in aid of charity. But Denis now says that he found it 'perfectly bloody, and not a bit funny'. Indeed the only thing that kept him in his seat was the fact that the whole occasion raised a huge sum for charity. I would like Denis to know that you don't have to see yourself on stage to find the play pretty tedious.

Incidentally, there is some confusion about Denis's golf handicap. I have talked to two separate people, one of whom says that it is 14, and the other who swears blind that Denis claims it to be 20. I can see four possibilities: Denis is pretending it is high from sheer modesty, or else in order to have a better chance of winning. Or he is pretending it is low in order to give his opponent more of a chance, or in order to make himself appear to be a better golfer than he is.

Prime Ministers really ought to make a point of being polite to their Backbenchers. If you habitually tread on people's toes as you climb the ladder, you can scarcely expect the same people to hold it steady for you while you're at the top. It's a lesson all party leaders ought to learn; one of the reasons why Jeremy Thorpe heard such a deafening silence from his fellow MPs when he was in trouble was because there was not one of them whom he had not insulted or mocked at one time or another.

Mrs Thatcher has been better with her backbenchers. An innocent young chap, the Member for some agreeable country town or tedious suburb, might be standing in the Division Lobby at around eight o'clock, his thoughts centred on a large, cold gin and tonic followed by a decent chop in the Members' Dining Room, when he is tapped on the shoulder. He spins around to see Mrs Thatcher's Parliamentary Private Secretary, Mr Ian Gow MP, known to all as 'Supergrass,' beaming at him with chilly benevolence. The Prime Minister would be pleased if you could join her for dinner. She would like to hear your views on the nuclear deterrent. . .' or the state of the economy, or elk-shooting for fun and profit.

The poor MP soon discovers that it is not his opinions which are being solicited, but hers which are being proferred. If he is wise, he will listen politely and will not disagree, however trivial the subject; remarks like, 'That's odd, we've always had marvellous weather in the Algarve,' will not be received well.

Nevertheless, however unnerving the occasion might be, and however scant the opportunities to present his own view of events, the MP does at least have the chance to meet his Leader. Tories grumble a great deal about Mrs Thatcher these days, but at least they never complain that they don't have access to her.

Eight years or so ago, Ted Heath found himself in a similarly difficult situation. His policies were going awry, the country was volubly unhappy and Tory MPs were openly complaining that they had little chance of winning the next election. One of Heath's closest confidants decided to mix metaphors and grasp the nettle by the horns. 'Ted,' he said, 'the problem is that you don't talk to the backbenchers enough. You must make them feel that you value their opinions and their judgement. You should go to the Smoking Room now and again, chat to them a while, be seen.'

He was rewarded by a blast of considered Heath invective. Didn't he know that Heath had far too much to do governing the country? Did he imagine that the Prime Minister could take time off in order to gossip with the drunks who inhabit the Smoking Room? And more of the same.

So the aide was particularly pleased when he went into the same Smoking Room a week later. For there, in the corner, busily chatting to a backbench MP, was Heath himself. The aide brought himself a drink, and carefully eased himself towards the two men, his ears straining to catch the Prime Minister's line of agreeable chatter. Then to his horror he heard Heath say: 'You do realise, don't you, that speech of yours the other day was perfectly *dreadful?*'

I've pointed out that many of the best known political quotations were never made by the people to whom they are attributed. Readers have sent in some more, and it's interesting to see that similar mistakes have been made for hundreds of years. It is, for example, almost certain that Wellington never said that the Battle of Waterloo had been won on the playing fields of Eton. The remark was attributed to him three years after his death by a Frenchman, who was referring to the school as a whole rather than its fields. In any case, Wellington loathed the place and never said anything complimentary about it.

When Marx wrote 'From each according to his abilities, to each according to his needs,' he put it in quotation marks, because he had probably lifted it from Saint-Simon. Nor did he ever write 'Workers of the World Unite, You Have Nothing To Lose But Your Chains,' though he did produce a similar, much longer, formulation. Neither George Bernard Shaw nor Sidney Webb (to both of whom I have seen it attributed) said, 'I have seen the future and it works.' But an obscure (and rather gullible) American journalist called Lincoln Steffens wrote of the USSR in 1919: 'I have been over into the future, and it works.'

And while we are at it, Charles Boyer never said, 'Come wiz me to the Casbah,' Humphrey Bogart did not say, 'Play it again, Sam,' James Cagney never in any of his films said, 'You dirty rat,' and, as I think is well known, Sherlock Holmes never ever, anywhere in the whole canon, uttered the words 'Elementary, my dear Watson.'

*The Prime Minister finally changed her Cabinet in
September 1981. They involved the dismissal of several
prominent 'Wets' and preferment for many 'Dries'.*

Mrs Thatcher has certainly promoted some tough customers in her Cabinet changes. Indeed the whole operation
has a touch of the Fuhrerbunker about it, with imaginary
divisions being shuffled about and old comrades shot for
speaking the truth. Possibly the Prime Minister has a poi-
son pellet waiting in case things get worse. If so, the pellet
is probably Mr Nigel Lawson, the new Secretary of State
for Energy, usually regarded as lethal even in minute doses.

A year or so ago I wrote an article about Mr Lawson
(nicknamed 'Niglet' by someone who is, curiously enough,
one of his greatest fans – Mr Norman St John-Stevas) in
which I mentioned one or two decisions he had been involved with in his days at the Treasury, adding: 'The Tory
Party divides into two groups about Mr Lawson; those
who hate him and those who loathe him.'

Next day Mr Lawson ran into one of my colleagues, to
whom he complained vigorously about the article. My
colleague agreed, saying that the item about 'loathing' had
been a little harsh. 'Oh, I don't mind that,' said Niglet.
'That's perfectly true. But the suggestion that I supported
the introduction of a tax on company perquisites is absolutely outrageous!'

The delegates who enjoyed the Liberal Party Assembly
most were the large numbers of deaf people who had been
invited. The Party, in a marvellously Liberal touch, em-
ployed a deaf and dumb sign language expert to signal the
debates from the platform throughout the whole conference. It must have been the first time that the narcoleptic
circumlocutions about decentralization and site value rating had ever been delivered by hand. Anyway, it was
completely new to deaf people who, like all the handi-
capped, are presumed to have no interest in politics. They
loved it and stayed for all the debates. But of course, with

the Liberals something always goes wrong. In the debate on disability, which included a chap with a terrible stammer and a fellow in a wheelchair, the blind speaker overran his time limit. So the chairman repeatedly flashed the red warning light in front of him on the rostrum.

What an immense pleasure to see Mr Geoffrey Dickens, Lothario of the *thé-dansants*, at Blackpool. Mr Dickens, the scourge of the paedophiles, was swigging heartily from a refreshing bottle of champagne. I was struck by this display of courage, since Mr Dickens recently had a frightening experience with a champagne bottle.

He and his wife Norma were attending the opening of a new headquarters for sea cadets in his constituency of Huddersfield. The wife of a lieutenant who had put a lot of effort into the new HQ had been asked to break a bottle of champagne over an anchor. She was worried that it

might not smash, so her husband had sliced round the bottom with a glass cutter. The bottle broke in the taxi on the way.

So when she came to crack the next bottle on the anchor, she hurled it with all the strength she could muster. The flagon did not merely break: it exploded with overwhelming force, drenching every fibre of Mr and Mrs Dickens's clothing and driving scores of glass fragments into every cranny and crevice. A lesser man might have eschewed champagne forever, but then lesser men are not made of the same stuff as Mr Dickens.

In October 1981, Granada began to show its epic TV serial, starring the Flyte family, the tedious Charles Ryder and Aloysius the teddy-bear.

It is now almost impossible for MPs to squeeze into the TV lounge on Tuesday nights, since it is already full of other MPs watching *Brideshead Revisited*. Some are Tories (and a few Socialists) re-living through misty eyes their Oxford past. Some are Labour MPs gloating at the disappearance of a privileged, decadent way of life. A few are just waiting for *News At Ten* to start.

I think that a deeper political truth may be discerned here. MPs can be divided up into Sebastians and Charleses. A Sebastian may be incapable of coping with life's rigours, but at heart he has a core of rust-proof self-esteem and assurance. In the long run he knows he will always be right. A Charles Ryder MP is simply looking for a Sebastian Flyte MP to admire.

Sir Ian Gilmour is a Sebastian. Mr St John-Stevas behaves like a Sebastian, but is really a Charles. Mr Healey is a Sebastian. Mr Eric Varley is a Charles. Michael Foot is most certainly a Charles, which is why he is perhaps not proving to be a particularly good leader of the Labour Party. All his Sebastians – Nye Bevan, Lord Beaverbrook and so forth – are long in their graves. Mr Whitelaw, though a well-to-do landed gent, is basically a Charles. Mr Heath, who is not from a wealthy background, is nevertheless a Sebastian, a trifle short on followers.

I put this theory to a Tory MP and asked him how he thought Sir Geoffrey Howe should be classified. 'As an Aloysius,' he said.

Parliament has its own slang, and one favourite word is 'bottom'. It means authority, seriousness, the ability to take the right decision among a shower of confusing facts and opinions. But it can sound peculiar in some contexts. I was chatting the other day to an SDP MP who was trying to sort out which of his colleagues he ought to support for Leader of the Party.

'I wonder,' he enquired, 'who has got more *bottom*, Shirley or Roy?' A tricky question, I'd say, but any impartial tailor must plump for Jenkins.

Just back from Salisbury, Zimbabwe, where the Parliament is another of those bizarre attempts dotted across the Empire to reproduce our own House of Commons. Since the elections in 1980, twenty of the seats are held by whites, all of them members of the Rhodesian Front, now renamed the Republican Front. The other eighty seats belong to black parties, and the great majority of the MPs and Ministers have never been near a legislative assembly in their lives.

The whites, who know very well that their small privileged reservation will not survive for long, have for the most part decided to see out the remnants of European rule by mercilessly taking the mickey out of their new black colleagues. Some of it is quite funny, though none of it is very encouraging for the new country.

A couple of months ago there was a long and acrimonious debate about training black technicians for Air Zimbabwe. This was being done by Air Ethiopia which, though a first-rate airline, was a source of much humour to the RF members. Mr Landau asked: 'Would the Minister agree that if it takes half as long to do a course for a pilot in Ethiopia as it does in Zimbabwe, then this is a crash course?'

The chief tormenter is Mr Donald Goddard, the white RF member for Lundi. He cheerfully describes his black colleagues as 'terrorists' and 'Communist-trained lackeys'. His speciality is using traditional parliamentary forms of speech to put over the racist jargon of the average Rhodie. 'Many of the Members in the Ministerial seats are proud of the fact that they have just come in from the Bush. I would respectfully suggest that is where they belong,' he said gravely.

Naturally, the new Ministers are forever getting confused about Second Readings and Committees of the Whole House and Supply Days, all of which furnishes more mirthful delight for the RF members. The supporters of Mr Mugabe and Mr Nkomo, having no knowledge or experience of parliaments, see their role not as tribunes of the people so much as cheerleaders for their parties (in which respect, perhaps, Zimbabwe is not all that different from Westminster).

I leave the last word with the ineffable Mr Goddard.
THE DEPUTY MINISTER FOR FOREIGN AFFAIRS: Is it in order, for an MP to point his finger at the Deputy Speaker?
MR DONALD GODDARD (RF, Lundi): If he is going to eat it, yes.

Like most recent by-elections, the one held in Crosby, Merseyside, was described as 'the by-election of the century'.

Mr Adrian Rossiter, the special assistant to Mrs Shirley Williams, appears to have created havoc throughout Crosby. He is, SDP staffers say, the exact opposite of her; while she is pleasant, agreeable, courteous and considerate, he isn't. Anyhow, the SDP people have now created a few neologisms from this young man's name. A rossit (n.) is an inflammation of the nostrils; to rossitate (vb., trans.) is to create an inflammation of the nostrils through perpendicular motion. It follows, therefore, that a rossiter (n.) is someone who gets right up your nose.

The hacks at the bv-election idled away some of the long hours by drawing up a cast list for the soon-to-be-filmed epic *Crosby!*. Shirley Williams will be played by Irene Handl, Roy Jenkins by Arthur Lowe, failed Tory candidate John Butcher by Derek Nimmo, and William Rodgers by the late Boris Karloff. Mr Adrian Rossiter will appear as himself.

I report a marvellously puzzled remark from Mr Geoffrey Dickens, the Lothario of *thé-dansants* who once held a press conference to announce that he had fallen in love with a woman not his wife. He had contemplated speaking in the controversial debate on law-and-order.

'I thought of putting my name down,' he said, 'but I didn't want people to think I was a self-publicist.'

There is a cry from the gut in a recent issue of *The House Magazine* which is, as its title implies, the Commons house magazine. A couple of MPs were asked to list their New Year's resolutions, and Julian Critchley, the Tory who sits for Aldershot, turned his into a long and entertaining wail about the horrors of life as a legislator.

'At Westminster I want nothing more than to lunch or dine in company that does not insist on talking about its ward boundaries . . . I will refuse to be bullied by my constituents. I shall send on enraged letters about Filipino dogs to Clement Freud, with a request for a recipe. I shall return to sender all letters written in green ink. I shall reserve for the curmudgeonly constituent cyclostyled replies which will read: "Dear Mr Jones, I wasted no time in reading your letter. . ." '

Mr Critchley's career was not exactly racing ahead when it came to a shuddering halt with the publication of an anonymous article attacking Mrs Thatcher in *The Observer*. It took the Whips about 24 hours to nail him as the culprit. Now he writes wryly: 'I shall cultivate gravitas and grow to look like Patrick Jenkin.'

Like many Tory MPs, Critchley has generally eschewed the weekly meeting of the 1922 Committee, which consists of all Conservative backbenchers discussing topics of the week. 'I may even break the habit of a lifetime and attend the '22. I shall not speak, however, being ever mindful of Walder's Law, propounded by the late David Walder, that "the first three people to speak on any subject are mad".'

He concludes: 'What should I look for in my stocking? An American research assistant who is more worth than she is trouble, an invitation to appear on *Desert Island Discs* ... and a pair who suffers from agoraphobia. Then indeed my cup would be full.'

The American research assistant is a wistful plea. There are many of these attractive and often highly intelligent people around the place, all prepared to do stacks of work for no money. I recall a certain Jewish MP being offered one. He was asked if he had any special requirements. 'Yes,' he said, 'She must be female, blonde and definitely not Jewish.' He got his wish.

In February 1982, Sally Oppenheim resigned as Prices Minister.

How sad it is to see Mrs Oppenheim depart from the Government. Generally when Ministers say that they are resigning for family reasons, it is a euphemism for something much more sinister. Confusingly, Mrs Oppenheim's motive appears to have been absolutely genuine. Perhaps she could have cleared things up by saying, 'I am obliged to resign my office because of the degrading scandal which hangs over my head and which, were I not to go, would occupy several Sunday newspaper front pages.' Then we would know that she was really going to look after her family.

Part of her unique fascination was the fact that she was in charge of consumer protection while being herself sumptuously rich. As Dennis Skinner once remarked on her knowledge (or lack of it) about the way working people live: 'The only shop floor she's ever known is at Fortnum & Mason.' She is something of a trencherwoman, and will plan a restaurant meal by first choosing her dessert, and then selecting appropriate entrée and main course to lead up to it.

John Fraser, the Labour MP who used to work opposite her during the Callaghan government, swears that she once told him briskly: 'The best form of consumer protection is to shop at Harrods.'

I have often written about the way well-known political quotations are almost invariably different from what was actually said in real life. Now I see an equally celebrated misquote has achieved universal currency less than six months after the original was first uttered. So let us see if we cannot stop it now. At no time, and as far as I know under no circumstances, has Mr Norman Tebbit, the Secretary of State for Employment, ever said 'on your bike', though I must have seen the phrase attributed to him a couple of dozen times. What he actually told the Tory conference in Blackpool last October was that his own father had been unemployed in the Thirties. 'But he did not riot. He got on his bike and looked for work.' As you can see, an entirely different remark.

THIS, HOWEVER, is not a misquotation: Mr Norman St John-Stevas's latest nickname for the Leader of his Party is 'the Immaculate Misconception'.

Fiction

☐	**Options**	Freda Bright	£1.50p
☐	**The Thirty-nine Steps**	John Buchan	£1.50p
☐	**Secret of Blackoaks**	Ashley Carter	£1.50p
☐	**Winged Victory**	Barbara Cartland	95p
☐	**The Sittaford Mystery**	Agatha Christie	£1.00p
☐	**Dupe**	Liza Cody	£1.25p
☐	**Lovers and Gamblers**	Jackie Collins	£2.25p
☐	**Sphinx**	Robin Cook	£1.25p
☐	**Ragtime**	E. L. Doctorow	£1.50p
☐	**Rebecca**	Daphne du Maurier	£1.75p
☐	**Flashman**	George Macdonald Fraser	£1.50p
☐	**The Moneychangers**	Arthur Hailey	£1.95p
☐	**Secrets**	Unity Hall	£1.50p
☐	**Simon the Coldheart**	Georgette Heyer	95p
☐	**The Eagle Has Landed**	Jack Higgins	£1.75p
☐	**The Master Sniper**	Stephen Hunter	£1.50p
☐	**Smiley's People**	John le Carré	£1.95p
☐	**To Kill a Mockingbird**	Harper Lee	£1.75p
☐	**The Empty Hours**	Ed McBain	£1.25p
☐	**Gone with the Wind**	Margaret Mitchell	£2.95p
☐	**The Totem**	Tony Morrell	£1.25p
☐	**Platinum Logic**	Tony Parsons	£1.75p
☐	**Wilt**	Tom Sharpe	£1.50p
☐	**Rage of Angels**	Sidney Sheldon	£1.75p
☐	**The Unborn**	David Shobin	£1.50p
☐	**A Town Like Alice**	Nevile Shute	£1.75p
☐	**A Falcon Flies**	Wilbur Smith	£1.95p
☐	**The Deep Well at Noon**	Jessica Stirling	£1.95p
☐	**The Ironmaster**	Jean Stubbs	£1.75p
☐	**The Music Makers**	E. V. Thompson	£1.50p

Non-fiction

☐	**Extraterrestrial Civilizations**	Isaac Asimov	£1.50p
☐	**Pregnancy**	Gordon Bourne	£2.95p
☐	**Out of Practice**	Rob Buckman	95p
☐	**The 35mm Photographer's Handbook**	Julian Calder and John Garrett	£5.95p
☐	**Travellers' Britain**	⎫ Arthur Eperon	£2.95p
☐	**Travellers' Italy**	⎭	£2.50p
☐	**The Complete Calorie Counter**	Eileen Fowler	70p

☐	**The Diary of Anne Frank**	Anne Frank	£1.25p
☐	**Linda Goodman's Sun Signs**	Linda Goodman	£1.95p
☐	**Mountbatten**	Richard Hough	£2.50p
☐	**How to be a Gifted Parent**	David Lewis	£1.95p
☐	**Symptoms**	Sigmund Stephen Miller	£2.50p
☐	**Book of Worries**	Robert Morley	£1.50p
☐	**The Hangover Handbook**	David Outerbridge edited by	£1.25p
☐	**The Alternative Holiday Catalogue**	Harriet Peacock	£1.95p
☐	**The Pan Book of Card Games**	Hubert Phillips	£1.75p
☐	**Food for All the Family**	Magnus Pyke	£1.50p
☐	**Everything Your Doctor Would Tell You If He Had the Time**	Claire Rayner	£4.95p
☐	**Just Off for the Weekend**	John Slater	£2.50p
☐	**An Unfinished History of the World**	Hugh Thomas	£3.95p
☐	**The Third Wave**	Alvin Toffler	£1.95p
☐	**The Flier's Handbook**		£5.95p

All these books are available at your local bookshop or newsagent, or
can be ordered direct from the publisher. Indicate the number of copies
required and fill in the form below   6

....

Name...
(Block letters please)

Address..

Send to Pan Books (CS Department), Cavaye Place, London SW10 9PG
Please enclose remittance to the value of the cover price plus:
35p for the first book plus 15p per copy for each additional book ordered
to a maximum charge of £1.25 to cover postage and packing
Applicable only in the UK

While every effort is made to keep prices low, it is sometimes
necessary to increase prices at short notice. Pan Books reserve
the right to show on covers and charge new retail prices which
may differ from those advertised in the text or elsewhere